Chocolate
Master Class

Frédéric Bau, Vincent Bourdin, Thierry Bridron, David Capy, Fabrice David, Philippe Givre,
Julie Haubourdin, Jérémie Runel, and Ève-Marie Zizza-Lalu all participated in the writing of this book.

All photographs are by Clay McLachlan, with the exception of pages 113 and 157: © Ginko.

Translated from the French by Carmella Abramowitz-Moreau
Design: Audrey Sednaoui
Layout: Artimon, Gilles Ittel
Editorial adaptation and additional translation: Anne McDowall
Typesetting: Gravemaker+Scott
Proofreading: Nicole Foster
Indexing: Cambridge Publishing Management Ltd
Color separation: IGS, Angoulême, France
Printed in China by Toppan Leefung

The majority of the recipes in this book were previously published in
Cooking with Chocolate: Essential Recipes and Techniques © Flammarion, S.A., Paris, 2011.

Originally published in French as *L'Essentiel du Chocolat*
© Flammarion, S.A., Paris, 2013

English-language edition
© Flammarion, S.A., Paris, 2014

87, quai Panhard et Levassor
75647 Paris Cedex 13

editions.flammarion.com

14 15 16 3 2 1

ISBN: 978-2-08-020201-7

Dépôt légal: 10/2014

Edited by Frédéric Bau • École du Grand Chocolat Valrhona
Photographs by Clay McLachlan

Chocolate Master Class

Essential Recipes and Techniques

With the collaboration of Julie Haubourdin

Flammarion

Contents

Preface

V alrhona is a French chocolate manufacturer that has been making exceptional gastronomic chocolate since 1922. Created by a pastry chef for pastry chefs, Valrhona has, for the last ninety years, devoted its skill, high standards, and passion to meeting the needs of culinary professionals, ensuring that each taste of its chocolate provides an unforgettable experience.

Selected by the world's best chefs and artisans for its vast aromatic range, which is regularly enhanced by innovative improvements, Valrhona seeks to promote pleasure and gastronomic fulfillment by offering different flavors of chocolate—unique and recognizable—that increasingly delight and surprise.

In a continuing effort to create a culture of dialogue and high ethical standards, Valrhona has built long-term collaborative relationships with planters and top chefs, and maintains a commitment to fair trade and environmental responsibility.

For more than twenty years, the École du Grand Chocolat Valrhona has been a catalyst for trends and has developed, cataloged, and preserved the expertise and techniques of the chocolate making profession. Its pastry chefs travel the world to meet professionals and exchange and disseminate skills, knowledge, and ideas as part of a permanent commitment to mutual development.

Techniques

Melting Chocolate

There are certain fundamental principles when melting chocolate, and if you follow them, your liquid chocolate will be ready to use as a base in all sorts of recipes. There are also two absolute no-no's. Firstly, don't put a spoonful of water in the pot; contrary to popular belief, it will not aid the melting process. Secondly, never cook chocolate over direct heat.

In a bain-marie

Using a serrated knife, chop the chocolate on a chopping board. You may also use couverture chocolate in other forms, such as fèves, buttons, or pistoles. Place the chopped chocolate in a glass or metal heatproof bowl.

If you have a double boiler, half fill the bottom part with hot water. Otherwise, half fill a pot or saucepan with hot water. Place the bowl in this, ensuring that it does not touch the bottom of the saucepan. Place the saucepan (or double boiler) over low heat and check that the water does not boil. As soon as the chocolate begins to melt, stir it continuously using a flexible rubber or silicone spatula so that it melts evenly.

In a microwave oven

Place the chocolate pieces in a bowl designed for microwave use. Heat at 500 W maximum for 1 minute, remove from the oven, stir with a flexible spatula, and return to the heat for 30 seconds.

Mix again and repeat the procedure as many times as necessary, until the chocolate has melted completely.

Tempering By Seeding

This tempering method uses the addition of finely chopped pieces, disks, or pistoles of chocolate into already melted chocolate. Adding stable, crystallized chocolate lowers the temperature naturally, enabling regular crystallization of the chocolate mass. The method is a replacement for using a marble working surface or a cold-water bath.

INGREDIENT

14 oz. (400 g) chocolate, ideally couverture chocolate in the form of fèves, buttons, or pistoles

EQUIPMENT

1 serrated knife
1 food processor fitted with a blade attachment (optional)
1 flexible spatula
1 kitchen thermometer

Chop three quarters of the chocolate (10 ½ oz./ 300 g) on a chopping board, using a serrated knife, or ideally use couverture chocolate in the form of fèves, buttons, or pistoles. Finely chop the remaining quarter (3 ½ oz./100 g) or process it with the blade knife attachment of a food processor. Place the roughly chopped chocolate in a bowl. Half fill a saucepan with hot water, and put the bowl over it, making sure that the bowl does not touch the bottom of the saucepan. Slowly heat the water, ensuring it does not boil.

Alternatively, use a microwave oven if you wish, but in "defrost" position or at 500 W maximum.

Stir regularly using a flexible spatula so that the chocolate melts smoothly. Check the temperature with a thermometer. When it reaches 131°F–136°F (55°C–58°C) for bittersweet, or 113°F–122°F (45°C– 50°C) for milk or white, remove the chocolate from the bain-marie. Set aside one third of the melted chocolate in a bowl, in a warm place. Add the remaining finely chopped quarter (3 ½ oz./100 g) of the chocolate into the remaining two thirds of the melted chocolate, stirring constantly.

Bittersweet chocolate should reach a temperature of 82°F–84°F (28°C–29°C); milk chocolate should reach 81°F–82°F (27°C–28°C); and white or colored chocolate should reach 79°F–81°F (26°C–27°C).

Then add the melted chocolate that you have set aside to increase the temperature. Bittersweet chocolate should reach 88°F–90°F (31°C–32°C); milk chocolate should reach 84°F–86°F (29°C–30°C); and white or colored chocolate should reach 82°F–84°F (28°C–29°C). Stir until the right temperature is reached.

Chef's note

If the chocolate has attained the right temperature and there are still pieces of unmelted chocolate, remove them before increasing the temperature. If you leave them, the chocolate will thicken very quickly and become sticky due to over-crystallization.

Tempering By Adding Cocoa Butter

INGREDIENTS

7 oz. (200 g) couverture chocolate
  (bittersweet, milk, white, or colored)
¾ teaspoon plus 7/64 teaspoon (1/14 oz./2 g) powdered
  cocoa butter

EQUIPMENT

1 weighing spoon
1 kitchen thermometer
1 flexible spatula

Melt the chocolate in a microwave oven or in a bain-marie to 104°F–113°F (40°C–45°C). Let the chocolate cool to 95°F (35°C) for bittersweet chocolate, or to room temperature for milk, white, or colored chocolate. Add 1 percent of cocoa butter (i.e., $^1/_{14}$ oz./2 g cocoa butter for 7 oz./200 g of chocolate).

Mix well using a flexible spatula and wait until the chocolate has cooled to 86°F (30°C) before using it.

Chef's note

Use a very precise weighing spoon to weigh the cocoa butter.

Why Temper Chocolate?

Tempering is the key to making small chocolates, bars, molded chocolate, and decorations. Merely melting a bar of chocolate is not enough for it to retain its qualities when used in another form, such as orangettes and mendiants. Only if the tempering is properly carried out will chocolate snap briskly, melt in the mouth pleasantly, and retain its gloss.

The reason for this is the large amount of cocoa butter present in chocolate. This fatty matter is complex and capricious. Insofar as a human attribute can be given to it, it can be described as "lazy"! Once it has melted, it cannot regain its stable crystalline form. This means that its component crystals are scattered. One result of this phenomenon is the "bloom"—the whitish streaks—you sometimes see on slabs of chocolate.

This is not only rather unattractive (where has that lovely sheen gone?) but also, and more importantly, you won't hear that distinctive snap when you break off a square of a good bar of chocolate, and it will be a big disappointment when you taste it. The chocolate will not melt gently, it may be grainy, and its aromas will not develop nearly as well. To avoid these mishaps, all you need to do is to help the cocoa butter regain the stable crystalline form that helps it keep well, and which will make it snap, melt, and shine.

In a nutshell, tempering is not merely a question of good looks, but, more importantly, of good taste.

Chef's note

To temper chocolate in the "classic" way, melt the chocolate to 131°F–136°F (55°C–58°C) for bittersweet chocolate or 113°F–122°F (45°C–50°C) for milk, white, or colored chocolate; to temper using cocoa butter, melt bittersweet, milk, or white chocolate to 104°F–113°F (40°C–45°C).

Classic Molding

INGREDIENT
Tempered chocolate, necessarily more than you'll need!
  (see pp. 13–15)

EQUIPMENT
Molds
2 confectionery rulers, cake cooling rack, or similar device
  to hold the mold upside down
1 baking sheet lined with parchment paper
1 large mixing bowl
1 ladle
1 kitchen knife
1 baking tray, warmed (optional)

Clean the molds using cotton wool and 90° alcohol. It's essential to remove all traces of grease from the molds so that the chocolate is unblemished when turned out of the mold.

Place the confectionery rulers on a baking sheet lined with parchment paper. Pour the tempered chocolate into a large mixing bowl. Dip a ladle into the tempered chocolate and completely fill the mold so that the entire surface is covered.

Turn it upside down over the mixing bowl to remove the excess chocolate. Drain it off by shaking the mold gently and then place it upside down over the two rulers.

When the chocolate begins to set, turn the mold over again and remove the excess chocolate by leveling it with a kitchen knife so that the edges are neat and trim.

If you are making larger pieces, you can thicken the chocolate by filling the molds a second time once you have leveled off the excess chocolate.

Trimming is important because it allows the chocolate to retract to the size of the mold and also facilitates your task when you turn your pieces out of their molds.

Chill for 30 minutes. When you remove the molds from the refrigerator, wait a few minutes before turning them out.

If you wish to mold your pieces together, slightly warm a baking tray or the bottom of a saucepan. Lightly melt the edges of your chocolate pieces against the warmed metal (if you are using a saucepan, turn it upside down) so that you can use the melted chocolate like glue.

Coating

Coating a chocolate bonbon involves enclosing a filling such as ganache, caramel, *pâte de fruit* (fruit jelly), and so on, in a fine layer of tempered chocolate. This technique helps to preserve the filling, adds a crisp texture, and enhances the chocolate taste.

INGREDIENTS
Tempered chocolate, necessarily more than you'll need!
  (see pp. 13–15)
Fillings for chocolate bonbons

EQUIPMENT
1 spatula (for uncut fillings) or pastry brush
  (for cut-out or molded fillings)
1 dipping fork
1 baking sheet lined with a sheet of food-safe acetate
  or parchment paper
1 chopstick (optional)

Undercoating

Firstly, undercoat the fillings to provide a protective layer and prevent fragile fillings from melting when they come into contact with the heat. Undercoating will also facilitate the handling of the fillings when you cut and coat them.

If undercoating before cutting the filling, spread a little tempered chocolate over the surface of your uncut filling, then using a spatula quickly spread the melted chocolate out into a very fine layer. This will form the base of the bonbon you are to coat. Cut it immediately into the desired shapes.

If undercoating molded fillings or after the filling has been cut into the desired shapes, use a pastry brush to spread a thin layer of tempered chocolate over the fillings.

Coating

Place the undercoated side of the bonbon on the tines of a dipping fork and dip it in the tempered chocolate. Lower the tines into the chocolate to immerse it completely. Use the fork to retrieve the bonbon, and dip it in three or four times to create the suction that will prevent an overly thick layer of chocolate from forming.

Scrape the dipping fork against the edge of the mixing bowl so that the layer of chocolate on the base is not too thick.

Carefully place the bonbon on the prepared baking sheet. If necessary, use a chopstick to slide it off the fork.

Chef's note

Clean the dipping fork and chopstick regularly. If they accumulate too much chocolate, the bonbons will stick, and it will be hard to slide them off.

Ganache for Hand-Dipped Centers

Ganache for hand-dipped bonbons, usually made in a confectionery frame (available at specialty stores and online), is the base for all sorts of coated chocolates: *palets d'or, rochers* ("rock" cookies), and lollipops are some examples. Its consistency is firmer than that of ganache for molded bonbons and it is easy to fashion, roll, and manipulate into various shapes.

INGREDIENTS

Weigh the chocolate according to its cocoa content:
Either 12 oz. (350 g) bittersweet chocolate, 70 percent cocoa
Or 13 oz. (370 g) bittersweet chocolate, 60 percent cocoa
Or 1 lb. 2 oz. (500 g) milk chocolate, 40 percent cocoa
Or 1 lb. 7 oz. (650 g) white chocolate, 35 percent cocoa
1 cup (250 ml) whipping cream
2 tablespoons (40 g) honey
5 tablespoons (2 ½ oz./70 g) butter, diced

EQUIPMENT

1 baking sheet lined with a sheet of food-safe acetate
1 confectionery frame or brownie pan (see Chef's note)
1 kitchen thermometer
1 flexible spatula
1 immersion blender
1 sheet of parchment paper

Line a baking sheet with a piece of food-safe acetate and place the confectionery frame over it.

Chop the chocolate and melt it slowly in a bain-marie or in the microwave oven (on "defrost" or at 500 W maximum, stirring from time to time).

Bring the whipping cream and honey to a boil in a saucepan. Slowly pour one third of the boiling mixture over the melted chocolate. Using a flexible spatula, briskly mix it in with a small circular movement to create an elastic, shiny "kernel." Then incorporate another third of the honey-cream mixture, using the same circular movement, and finally, the last third, still mixing with a circular movement.

As soon as the ganache reaches a temperature of 95°F–104°F (35°C–40°C), add the diced butter.

Process with an immersion blender to ensure that the mixture is smooth and forms a perfect emulsion. Immediately pour it into the frame. This type of ganache should ideally be stored at 61°F–64°F (16°C–18°C) while it sets.

Leave to set for 12 hours, then turn it out onto a sheet of parchment paper. Remove the frame and the acetate sheet. Undercoat (see p. 18) and cut into the desired shapes; leave to set for another 24 hours. Coat with tempered chocolate (see p. 18).

Chef's note

If you don't have a confectionery frame, use a brownie pan or dish just deep enough to pour your ganache to a thickness of under ½ in. (1 cm). Oil it and line with smoothed-out plastic wrap.

Chocolate Cake Batter

**Unsweetened cocoa powder, which tastes bitter,
can be used in cakes to give them a dark, rich color.**

INGREDIENTS
2 ½ oz. (70 g) bittersweet chocolate, 70 percent cocoa
1 stick (4 ¼ oz./120 g) butter
1 ¾ cups (5 ½ oz./160 g) cake flour
2 ½ teaspoons (10 g) baking powder
¼ cup (1 oz./30 g) unsweetened cocoa powder
6 eggs
Scant ⅓ cup (3 ½ oz./100 g) acacia honey
Scant cup (6 oz./170 g) granulated sugar
1 cup plus 3 tablespoons (3 ½ oz./100 g) ground almonds
⅔ cup (160 ml) whipping cream
Scant ⅓ cup (70 ml) rum

EQUIPMENT
1 loaf pan, 10 in. (25 cm)
Parchment paper
1 sieve
1 whisk

Preheat the oven to 300°F (150°C). Line the loaf pan with parchment paper. Chop the chocolate and dice the butter. Melt the chocolate and butter slowly in a bain-marie or in the microwave oven (on "defrost" or at 500 W maximum, stirring from time to time).

Sift the flour with the baking powder and cocoa powder. Whisk the eggs, honey, and sugar together in a mixing bowl. Stir in the ground almonds and the sifted dry ingredients and add the cream. Incorporate the melted chocolate and butter, and then the rum until just mixed through.

Pour the batter into the prepared pan. Bake for about 40 minutes, or until a cake tester or knife tip comes out clean.

Chef's note
You can also bake this batter on a jelly (Swiss) roll pan, in which case you should bake it at 350°F (180°C) for about 10 minutes. Use this method to cut out bases and layers for desserts.

Egg White–Based Chocolate Mousse

This is the chocolate mousse our grandmothers used to treat us with. Airy and rich in chocolate, it gives a sensation of gently melting in the mouth.

INGREDIENTS

Weigh the chocolate according to its cocoa content:

Either 10 ½ oz. (300 g) bittersweet chocolate, 70 percent cocoa

Or 11 ⅔ oz. (330 g) bittersweet chocolate, 60 percent cocoa

Or 13 ¾ oz. (390 g) milk chocolate, 40 percent cocoa, plus 1 ½ sheets (3 g) gelatin

Or 13 ¾ oz. (390 g) milk chocolate, 35 percent cocoa, plus 3 sheets (6 g) gelatin

Scant ⅔ cup (150 ml) whipping cream

3 (2 ⅛ oz./60 g) egg yolks

6–7 (7 oz./200 g) egg whites

¼ cup (1 ¾ oz./50 g) granulated sugar

EQUIPMENT

1 whisk or flexible spatula

1 immersion blender

1 kitchen thermometer

1 handheld electric beater or stand-alone mixer

Chop the chocolate and melt it slowly in a bain-marie or in the microwave oven (on "defrost" or at 500 W maximum, stirring from time to time). If you are using milk or white chocolate, soften the gelatin in very cold water. Bring the cream to a boil in a saucepan, then remove from the heat. Wring the water out of the gelatin, if using, and dissolve it into the cream.

Slowly pour one third of the hot cream over the melted chocolate. Using a whisk or flexible spatula, briskly mix it in with a small circular movement to create an elastic, shiny "kernel." Then incorporate another third, using the same movement, and finally, the last third, still mixing as before. Beat in the egg yolks. Process with an immersion blender to ensure that the mixture is smooth and perfectly emulsified.

In the meantime, start whisking the egg whites with the sugar with a handheld electric beater or in the bowl of a stand-alone mixer until they form soft peaks. When the chocolate mixture cools to 95°F–113°F (35°C–45°C) for white or milk chocolate, or 113°F–122°F (45°C–50°C) for bittersweet chocolate, fold in a quarter of the whisked egg whites, then carefully fold in the rest.

Pour into individual serving bowls.

Chill for 12 hours.

Chef's note

This mousse will only keep for up to 24 hours because of the raw egg yolks.

Egg-Free Chocolate Mousse

**This is an extremely light mousse that uses milk and gelatin.
It should be eaten straight from the refrigerator.**

INGREDIENTS
Weigh the chocolate according to its cocoa content:
Either 10 oz. (285 g) bittersweet chocolate, 70 percent
  cocoa, plus 1 ½ sheets (3 g) gelatin
Or 11 ⅔ oz. (330 g) bittersweet chocolate, 60 percent
  cocoa, plus 2 sheets (4 g) gelatin
Or 12 oz. (340 g) milk chocolate, 40 percent cocoa, plus
  2 ½ sheets (5 g) gelatin
Or 1 lb. ½ oz. (470 g) white chocolate, 35 percent cocoa,
  plus 5 sheets (10 g) gelatin
1 cup (250 ml) whole milk
2 cups (500 ml) whipping cream, well chilled

EQUIPMENT
1 flexible spatula
1 whisk or handheld electric beater
1 kitchen thermometer

Chop the chocolate and melt it slowly in a bain-marie or in the microwave oven (on "defrost" or at 500 W maximum, stirring from time to time).

Soften the gelatin in a bowl of very cold water.

Bring the milk to a boil in a saucepan. Wring the water out of the gelatin and incorporate it into the hot milk. Immediately remove from the heat.

Slowly pour one third of the hot mixture over the melted chocolate. Using a flexible spatula, briskly mix it in with a small circular movement to create an elastic, shiny "kernel." Then incorporate another third of the hot liquid, using the same circular movement, and finally, the last third, still mixing with a circular movement.

Using either a whisk or an electric beater, whisk the well-chilled cream until it is lightly whipped.

When the chocolate mixture reaches 95°F–113°F (35°C–45°C) for white or milk chocolate, or 113°F–122°F (45°C–50°C) for bittersweet chocolate, fold in the lightly whipped cream carefully with a flexible spatula. Chill for at least 12 hours.

Chef's notes
This mousse is ideal for people who are allergic to eggs. It keeps for 1 to 2 days in the refrigerator and can be frozen.

Chocolate Crémeux

Adding chocolate to the basic *crémeux* recipe makes for a perfect base that will allow you to create delicious, multi-textured desserts.

INGREDIENTS

Weigh the chocolate according to its cocoa content:
Either 6 ¾ oz. (190 g) bittersweet chocolate, 70 percent cocoa
Or 7 ½ oz. (210 g) bittersweet chocolate, 60 percent cocoa
Or 9 oz. (250 g) milk chocolate, 40 percent cocoa
Or 8 oz. (225 g) white chocolate, 35 percent cocoa, plus 1 ½ sheets (3 g) gelatin
5 egg yolks
¼ cup (1 ¾ oz./50 g) granulated sugar
1 cup (250 ml) whole milk
1 cup (250 ml) whipping cream

EQUIPMENT

1 kitchen thermometer
1 whisk or handheld electric beater
1 immersion blender
1 flexible spatula
Plastic wrap

The day before the *crémeux* will be used, melt the chocolate slowly in a bain-marie or in the microwave oven (on "defrost" or at 500 W maximum, stirring from time to time).

Soften the gelatin in cold water if you are using white chocolate. Whip the egg yolks and sugar together until thick and pale. Pour the mixture into a saucepan with the milk and cream and cook over low heat until it coats the back of a spoon and is slightly thickened. The temperature should be between 82°F and 84°F (28°C–29°C).

Wring the water out of the gelatin sheets and incorporate it at this stage. Remove the saucepan from the heat and pour the custard into a deep bowl. Process for a few seconds with an immersion blender until the texture is smooth and creamy. Slowly pour one third of the hot custard over the melted chocolate. Using a flexible spatula, energetically mix one third of the cream into the chocolate, drawing small, quick circles in the center to create a shiny, elastic "kernel." Incorporate the second third and mix in the same way. Pour in the remaining third, again using the same stirring technique. Use an immersion blender to finish the emulsifying process.

Pour it into a bowl and cover with plastic wrap flush with the surface to prevent a skin from forming. Chill overnight.

Chocolate Pastry Cream

This is the star ingredient of chocolate éclairs. This recipe makes enough to fill at least 10 éclairs (1–1 ½ oz. or 30–40 g per éclair).

INGREDIENTS
Either 3 oz. (85 g) bittersweet chocolate, 70 percent cocoa
Or 3 ½ oz. (95 g) bittersweet chocolate, 60 percent cocoa
2 egg yolks
1 tablespoon (⅓ oz./10 g) cornstarch
2 ½ tablespoons (1 oz./30 g) granulated sugar
Scant cup (220 ml) whole milk
Scant ¼ cup (50 ml) whipping cream

EQUIPMENT
1 whisk
1 flexible spatula (optional)
1 immersion blender

Chop the chocolate and melt it slowly in a bain-marie or in the microwave oven (on "defrost" or at 500 W maximum, stirring from time to time).

Whisk the egg yolks with the cornstarch and sugar until thick and pale.

Bring the milk and cream to a boil. Pour a little into the egg yolks combined with the dry ingredients and mix thoroughly. Return the saucepan to the heat. Pour the diluted egg mixture into the saucepan and cook over low heat, stirring constantly with a whisk until it thickens. Continue cooking for a few more minutes, still stirring so that the cream does not stick to the bottom of the saucepan. It should become creamier; most importantly, it must be shiny.

Slowly pour one third of the hot cream over the melted chocolate. Using a whisk or flexible spatula, mix in energetically, drawing small circles to create an elastic, shiny "kernel."

Incorporate the second third of the liquid, using the same procedure. Repeat with the last third.

Blend briefly using an immersion blender so that the mixture is smooth and perfectly emulsified.

Chocolate Sauce

Chocolate sauce enhances everything. It's the finishing touch for a number of iced desserts and is the indispensable ingredient in many classic dishes, drizzled over Poire Belle Hélène, banana splits, and profiteroles. The quality of your chocolate makes all the difference, so use the best you can.

INGREDIENTS
Weigh the chocolate according to its cocoa content:
Either 3 oz. (85 g) bittersweet chocolate, 70 percent cocoa
Or 3 ¼ oz. (90 g) bittersweet chocolate, 60 percent cocoa
Or 4 ¾ oz. (130 g) milk chocolate, 40 percent cocoa
Or 5 oz. (140 g) white chocolate, 35 percent cocoa
Scant ½ cup (100 ml) whole milk

EQUIPMENT
1 flexible spatula
1 immersion blender
1 kitchen thermometer

Chop the chocolate and melt it slowly in a bain-marie or in the microwave oven (on "defrost" or at 500 W maximum, stirring from time to time).

Bring the milk to a boil.

Gradually pour one third of the boiling milk over the melted chocolate. Using a flexible spatula, mix in energetically, drawing small circles to create an elastic, shiny "kernel."

Incorporate the second third of the milk, using the same procedure. Repeat with the last third.

Blend for a few seconds using an immersion blender. Serve hot, or reserve in the refrigerator.

Milk and white chocolate sauce should be served at 68°F–77°F (20°C–25°C); bittersweet chocolate should be served at 95°F–104°F (35°C–40°C).

Chef's note
If you wish, you may sweeten bittersweet chocolate sauce by adding a little milk chocolate or sugar.

A Craving for Something . . .

Velvety

Molten Chocolate Cakes

SERVES 6–8 · PREPARATION TIME: 20 MINUTES · COOKING TIME: 10–12 MINUTES

INGREDIENTS

4 ½ oz. (125 g) bittersweet chocolate, 70 percent cocoa
7 tablespoons (3 ½ oz./100 g) butter, plus a little extra
  to grease the molds
4 eggs
¾ cup (5 ¼ oz./145 g) granulated sugar
Generous ½ cup (1 ¾ oz./50 g) cake flour

EQUIPMENT

6–8 molds, 2 ½–3 in. (6–8 cm) diameter
1 whisk or handheld electric beater
1 sieve

Butter the molds and line them with parchment paper. Preheat the oven to 375°F (190°C).

Chop the chocolate and melt it slowly in a bain-marie or in the microwave oven (on "defrost" or at 500 W maximum, stirring from time to time). Stir in the butter.

Whisk the eggs with the sugar until pale and thick. Add the chocolate–butter mixture, then sift in the flour. Stir until just combined and pour into the molds.

Bake for 10–12 minutes. Turn the cakes out onto plates and serve immediately.

Mini Molten Chocolate Cakes with Banana *Verrines*

SERVES 6–8 · PREPARATION TIME: 1 HOUR 40 MINUTES · CHILLING TIME: OVERNIGHT
FREEZING TIME: OVERNIGHT · COOKING TIME: 15 MINUTES

INGREDIENTS

Molten chocolate cakes
5 ⅔ oz. (160 g) bittersweet chocolate, 70 percent cocoa
1 ⅓ sticks (5 ⅔ oz./160 g) butter, plus a little extra for greasing the pastry rings
5–6 eggs, total weight 10 oz. (280 g)
⅔ cup (4 ½ oz./125 g) sugar
Scant cup (2 ¾ oz./80 g) cake flour

Chocolate granita
Either 6 oz. (170 g) bittersweet chocolate, 70 percent cocoa
Or 6 ¾ oz. (190 g) bittersweet chocolate, 60 percent cocoa

2 ¾ cups (650 ml) water
1 ½ tablespoons (⅓ oz./10 g) powdered milk
⅔ cup (4 ½ oz./125 g) sugar
1 heaped tablespoon (1 oz./25 g) honey

Softened bananas
1 tablespoon (½ oz./15 g) butter
2 passion fruit
2 or 3 bananas, total weight approx. 8 oz. (240 g)
1 ½ tablespoons (⅔ oz./20 g) brown sugar
¼ cup (60 ml) orange juice
2 grinds of the pepper mill with Sarawak pepper

1 quantity almond streusel (see p. 187) or 1 packet shortbread cookies

EQUIPMENT
1 whisk or handheld electric beater
1 flexible spatula
1 immersion blender
Individual pastry rings 2–2 ¼ in. (5–6 cm) diameter, 2 in. (5 cm) high
1 baking sheet lined with parchment paper
1 piping bag
8 shot glasses or small bowls

A day ahead, prepare the chocolate cakes.
Chop the chocolate and melt it slowly in a bain-marie or in the microwave oven (on "defrost" or at 500 W maximum, stirring from time to time). Add the butter and stir until thoroughly combined and smooth. Beat the eggs and sugar until thick and pale, and then stir in the flour. Stir the chocolate into the eggs and sugar and chill overnight.

Prepare the chocolate granita.
Chop the chocolate and melt it slowly in a bain-marie or in the microwave oven (on "defrost" or at 500 W maximum, stirring from time to time).
Heat the water, powdered milk, sugar, and honey in a saucepan and leave to simmer for 2 minutes. Gradually pour one third of the syrup mixture over the melted chocolate. Using a flexible spatula, mix in energetically, drawing small circles to create an elastic, shiny "kernel." Incorporate the second third of the liquid, using the same procedure. Repeat with the last third. Blend for a few seconds using an immersion blender so that the mixture is smooth and perfectly emulsified. Pour it into a dish to just over 1 in. (3 cm) thick. Place in the freezer overnight, stirring or scraping regularly to form crystals that are just the right size.

The next day, prepare the softened bananas.
Preheat the oven to 400°F (200°C). Melt the butter in the microwave oven. Cut open the passion fruit and extract the juice and, if you wish, the seeds. Peel the bananas and slice them into rounds that are not too thin. Combine the melted butter, brown sugar, orange and passion fruit juice, and pepper. Pour this marinade over the bananas and stir to combine. Place in an ovenproof dish and bake for 6 to 8 minutes. Set aside at room temperature.

Prepare the almond streusel (see p. 187) if using, or crumble the shortbread cookies.
Preheat the oven to 375°F (190°C). Remove the chocolate batter from the refrigerator and warm it up briefly in the microwave oven at 500 W. Grease the pastry rings with softened butter and place

them on a baking sheet lined with parchment paper. Spoon the batter into a piping bag and pipe it out into the rings. Bake for 6 to 7 minutes. While they are baking, arrange the softened bananas in the glasses and spoon the chocolate granita over the top. Garnish with a few pieces of streusel or crumbed cookies. Place in the freezer.

Remove the molten chocolate cakes from the oven, wait for about 30 seconds, then turn them out onto plates. Serve accompanied by the iced *verrines*.

Homemade Chocolate Spread

SERVES 6–8 · PREPARATION TIME: 30 MINUTES · COOKING TIME: 10 MINUTES

INGREDIENTS
¼ cup (1 ½ oz./40 g) whole blanched almonds
1 cup (5 ⅔ oz./160 g) whole hazelnuts
1 ¾ cups (400 ml) whole milk
½ cup (2 ¼ oz./60 g) powdered milk
2 tablespoons (1 ½ oz./40 g) honey
5 ½ oz. (150 g) milk chocolate, 40 percent cocoa
Either 5 ½ oz. (150 g) bittersweet chocolate,
  60 percent cocoa
Or 5 oz. (140 g) bittersweet chocolate, 70 percent cocoa

EQUIPMENT
1 food processor
1 chinois (fine sieve)
Glass jars

Preheat the oven to 300°F (150°C). Place the almonds and hazelnuts in the oven and roast until they are a nice amber color right through. This should take about 10 minutes.

Leave them to cool, then rub the hazelnuts between your hands to remove the skins. Grind the almonds and hazelnuts in the bowl of a food processor until they are reduced to a paste.

Combine the milk, powdered milk, and honey in a saucepan and bring the mixture to a boil.

Chop up the milk and bittersweet chocolates and melt both slowly in a bain-marie or in the microwave oven (on "defrost" or at 500 W maximum, stirring from time to time).

Add the melted chocolate to the nut paste in the food processor and pour in the boiling milk—honey mixture. Process briefly. Strain the mixture through a chinois (fine sieve) and pour it into jars.

Chocolate Cream with Jelled Coffee

SERVES 8 · PREPARATION TIME: 20 MINUTES · COOKING TIME: 12 MINUTES
CHILLING TIME: 2 HOURS 30 MINUTES

INGREDIENTS

Chocolate cream
Either 5 oz. (140 g) bittersweet chocolate, 60 percent cocoa
Or 4 ¼ oz. (120 g) bittersweet chocolate, 70 percent cocoa
Scant ½ cup (100 ml) milk
1 egg
1 egg yolk

Jelled coffee
1 sheet (2 g) gelatin
Scant ½ cup (100 ml) strong espresso coffee

EQUIPMENT

1 flexible spatula
1 whisk or handheld electric beater
8 shot glasses or small bowls
Plastic wrap
1 steamer basket or couscous pot with colander

Prepare the chocolate creams.

Chop the chocolate and melt it slowly in a bain-marie or in the microwave oven (on "defrost" or at 500 W maximum, stirring from time to time). Heat the milk in a saucepan, removing it from the heat just before it comes to a boil. Gradually pour one third of the hot milk over the melted chocolate. Using a flexible spatula, mix it in energetically, drawing small circles to create an elastic, shiny "kernel." Incorporate the second third of the liquid, using the same procedure. Repeat with the last third until the mixture is quite smooth and creamy. Beat the egg and extra yolk together and stir into the chocolate mixture.

Pour the cream into the small glasses or bowls and cover them with plastic wrap. Place them in a steamer basket or colander. Put them over gently simmering water, cover the pot with the lid, and cook for 10 to 12 minutes. This is the time required for a glass with a diameter of 2 in. (5 cm) containing just over 1 in. (3 cm) of cream. The cream is done when the surface offers a little resistance to the touch; the interior should not be liquid.

Immediately chill the creams by placing them in a bowl of ice water and then leave to set in the refrigerator.

Prepare the jelled coffee.

Soften the gelatin in a bowl of cold water. Prepare a scant ½ cup (100 ml) of very strong coffee, preferably espresso. Wring the water out of the gelatin and incorporate it into the hot coffee until it is dissolved. Pour it into a small dish so that it is just under ½ in. (1 cm) deep. Chill for at least 2 hours, until quite set. Cut into small dice.

Serve the chocolate creams well chilled and accompany with the small cubes of jelled coffee.

Traditional Hot Chocolate

SERVES 6 · PREPARATION TIME: 10 MINUTES · COOKING TIME: 10 MINUTES

INGREDIENTS

3 cups plus scant ½ cup (850 ml) whole
  or reduced-fat milk
1 tablespoon unsweetened cocoa powder
6 ½ oz. (185 g) bittersweet chocolate, 70 percent cocoa

EQUIPMENT

1 whisk

Bring the milk to a boil with the cocoa powder.

Chop the chocolate and melt it slowly in a bain-marie or in the microwave oven (on "defrost" or at 500 W maximum, stirring from time to time).

Pour one third of the boiling cocoa-flavored milk over the melted chocolate, whisking as you do so, until the texture is smooth, elastic, and shiny. Pour in the remaining liquid, whisking continuously.

Return the liquid to the heat, whisking energetically to form a light, creamy foam with small, compact air bubbles.

Almond-Flavored Hot Chocolate

SERVES 6 · PREPARATION TIME: 15 MINUTES · COOKING TIME: 10 MINUTES

INGREDIENTS

3 cups plus generous ⅓ cup (840 ml) whole or
  reduced-fat milk
1 ¾ oz. (50 g) almond paste (see p. 186, or buy from
  specialty stores or online)
5 ⅔ oz. (160 g) bittersweet chocolate, 60–70 percent cocoa

EQUIPMENT

1 whisk

Bring the milk to a boil. To soften the almond paste, place it in the microwave oven on low power (400 to 500 W) for about 40 seconds. Blend it with the milk.

Chop the chocolate and melt it slowly in a bain-marie or in the microwave oven (on "defrost" or at 500 W maximum, stirring from time to time).

Pour one third of the boiling liquid over the melted chocolate, whisking as you do so, until the texture is smooth, elastic, and shiny. Pour in the remaining liquid, whisking continuously.

Return the liquid to the heat, whisking energetically to form a light, creamy foam with small, compact air bubbles.

Spiced Hot Chocolate

SERVES 6 · PREPARATION TIME: 20 MINUTES · COOKING TIME: 10 MINUTES

INGREDIENTS

4 cups (1 liter) whole or reduced-fat milk

Scant teaspoon (2 g) mixed spices (either store-bought or homemade), containing star anise, nutmeg (or mace), cardamom, cloves, cinnamon, and ginger

2 sticks cinnamon

3 ½ oz. (100 g) bittersweet chocolate, 60 percent cocoa

3 ½ oz. (100 g) milk chocolate, 40 percent cocoa

EQUIPMENT

1 chinois (fine sieve)

1 whisk

Bring the milk to a boil with the spices. Remove from the heat and leave to infuse for a few minutes, then remove the cinnamon sticks and strain the spiced milk through a chinois (fine sieve).

Chop the chocolate and melt it slowly in a bain-marie or in the microwave oven (on "defrost" or at 500 W maximum, stirring from time to time).

Pour one third of the boiling liquid over the melted chocolate, whisking as you do so, until the texture is smooth, elastic, and shiny. Pour in the remaining liquid, whisking continuously.

Return the liquid to the heat, whisking energetically to form a light, creamy foam with small, compact air bubbles.

Earl Grey–Scented Hot Chocolate

SERVES 6 · PREPARATION TIME: 20 MINUTES · COOKING TIME: 10 MINUTES

INGREDIENTS

3 cups plus 1 scant ¼ cup (800 ml) whole or
 reduced-fat milk
¾ cup (200 ml) whipping cream
2 tablespoons (⅓ oz./10 g) Earl Grey tea leaves
6 ⅓ oz. (180 g) bittersweet chocolate, 65 percent cocoa

EQUIPMENT

1 chinois (fine sieve)
1 whisk

Bring the milk and the cream to a boil. Add the Earl Grey tea leaves and let infuse for a few minutes, then strain through a chinois (fine sieve).

Chop the chocolate and melt it slowly in a bain-marie or in the microwave oven (on "defrost" or at 500 W maximum, stirring from time to time).

Pour one third of the boiling liquid over the melted chocolate, whisking as you do so, until the texture is smooth, elastic, and shiny. Pour in the remaining liquid, whisking continuously.

Return the liquid to the heat, whisking energetically to form a light, creamy foam with small, compact air bubbles.

Hazelnut-Flavored Hot Chocolate

SERVES 6 · **PREPARATION TIME: 10 MINUTES** · **COOKING TIME: 10 MINUTES**

INGREDIENTS

3 cups plus 1 scant ¼ cup (800 ml) whole or
 reduced-fat milk
¾ cup (200 ml) whipping cream
⅔ oz. (20 g) hazelnut paste (see p. 188, or buy from
 specialty stores or online)
9 oz. (250 g) milk chocolate, 40 percent cocoa

EQUIPMENT

1 whisk

Bring the milk, cream, and hazelnut paste to a boil and stir well to mix.

Chop the chocolate and melt it slowly in a bain-marie or in the microwave oven (on "defrost" or at 500 W maximum, stirring from time to time).

Gradually pour one third of the boiling liquid over the melted chocolate, whisking as you do so, until the texture is smooth, elastic, and shiny. Pour in the remaining liquid, whisking continuously.

Return the liquid to the heat, whisking energetically to form a light, creamy foam with small, compact air bubbles.

Cafe con Choco

SERVES 6–8 · PREPARATION TIME: 15 MINUTES · CHILLING TIME: 1–2 HOURS · COOKING TIME: 10 MINUTES

INGREDIENTS
3 ½ oz. (100 g) bittersweet chocolate, 70 percent cocoa
1 ½ oz. (40 g) milk chocolate, 40 percent cocoa
2 cups (500 ml) whole milk
1 ¼ cups (300 ml) espresso coffee
Ice cubes

EQUIPMENT
1 flexible spatula
1 chinois (fine sieve)
1 shaker

Chop the bittersweet and milk chocolate and melt it slowly in a bain-marie or in the microwave oven (on "defrost" or at 500 W maximum, stirring from time to time).

Bring the milk to a boil. Gradually pour one third of the boiling liquid over the melted chocolate. Using a flexible spatula, mix in energetically, drawing small circles to create an elastic, shiny "kernel." Incorporate the second third of the liquid, using the same procedure. Repeat with the last third. Strain through a chinois (fine sieve) and chill.

When the chocolate is cold, prepare the espresso coffee and pour it into a shaker. Add ice cubes, cool, and shake the coffee to foam. Pour the cold chocolate into the shaker and shake again.

To serve, add ice cubes to the glasses.

Teh Tarik with Chocolate

SERVES 6 · PREPARATION TIME: 20 MINUTES · COOKING TIME: 10 MINUTES

INGREDIENTS
5 oz. (140 g) bittersweet chocolate, 70 percent cocoa
2 cups (500 ml) water
2 ½ tablespoons (1 oz./25 g) Pu-Erh tea,
  or other fine black tea
¼ cup (60 ml) sweetened condensed milk

EQUIPMENT
1 chinois (fine sieve)
1 whisk
1 immersion blender or blender

Chop the chocolate and melt it slowly in a bain-marie or in the microwave oven (on "defrost" or at 500 W maximum, stirring from time to time).

Heat the water until it is simmering. Pour it over the tea leaves and leave to infuse for 5 minutes, then strain through a chinois (fine sieve).

Pour one third of the hot tea over the melted chocolate, whisking so that you have a smooth, elastic, and shiny texture. Then pour in the remaining liquid, whisking continuously.

Lastly, add the cold sweetened condensed milk, and process it with an immersion blender or in the blender to make a nice foam.

Serve immediately.

Milky Chocolate Jelly

SERVES 6–8 · PREPARATION TIME: 40–60 MINUTES · COOKING TIME: 30 MINUTES

INGREDIENTS
½ vanilla bean
3 ¼ cups (800 ml) whole milk
¾ cup (200 ml) whipping cream
1 ½ cups (10 ½ oz./300 g) granulated sugar
7 tablespoons (5 ½ oz./150 g) glucose syrup
2 ½ tablespoons (1 ¾ oz./50 g) honey
3 ½ oz. (100 g) milk chocolate, 40 percent cocoa

EQUIPMENT
Small jelly jars
1 kitchen thermometer

Sterilize your jars before using them: leave them in a 200°F (90°C–95°C) oven for 20 minutes.

Slit the half vanilla bean lengthwise and scrape out the seeds into the milk. Bring the milk, cream, sugar, glucose syrup, vanilla seeds and bean, and honey to a boil. Leave to simmer for about 30 minutes, until the mixture caramelizes slightly and coats the back of a spoon. The temperature at this stage will be about 215°F–217°F (102°C–103°C). Remove the vanilla bean.

Chop the chocolate and melt it slowly in a bain-marie or in the microwave oven (on "defrost" or at 500 W maximum, stirring from time to time). Stir the melted chocolate into the milk mixture.

Fill the pots immediately with the hot mixture and place in the refrigerator. Keeps for 1 week.

Bittersweet Chocolate Fondue

SERVES 6–8 · PREPARATION TIME: 40 MINUTES

INGREDIENTS
Generous ¾ cup (210 ml) milk
½ cup plus 2 tablespoons (150 ml) whipping cream
1 tablespoon (⅔ oz./20 g) glucose syrup
1 tablespoon (⅔ oz./20 g) honey
½ vanilla bean
13 ¼ oz. (375 g) bittersweet chocolate,
    70 percent cocoa

To serve
Marshmallows
Fruit jellies
Macaroons
Pieces of fresh fruit

EQUIPMENT
1 flexible spatula
1 kitchen thermometer

Bring the milk to a boil with the cream, glucose syrup, and honey. Slit the half vanilla bean lengthwise and scrape out the seeds. Leave the bean and seeds to infuse in the hot mixture.

Chop the chocolate and melt it slowly in a bain-marie or in the microwave oven (on "defrost" or at 500 W maximum, stirring from time to time). Gradually pour one third of the boiling liquid over the melted chocolate. Using a flexible spatula, mix in energetically, drawing small circles to create an elastic, shiny "kernel." Incorporate the second third of the liquid, using the same procedure. Repeat with the last third.

Pour the fondue into bowls and chill, or use immediately at a temperature between 108°F–113°F (42°C–45°C). Serve with marshmallows, fruit jellies, macaroons, or pieces of fresh fruit, to be dipped in the fondue.

Truffle Hearts

SERVES 8 · PREPARATION TIME: 1 HOUR · CHILLING TIME: 3 HOURS

INGREDIENTS

Bittersweet chocolate ganache
8 oz. (225 g) bittersweet chocolate, 70 percent cocoa
½ vanilla bean
¾ cup (200 ml) whipping cream
2 tablespoons (1 ½ oz./40 g) acacia honey
3 ½ tablespoons (1 ¾ oz./50 g) butter, diced

Coating
10 ½ oz. (300 g) bittersweet chocolate, 70 percent cocoa
Unsweetened cocoa powder for dusting

EQUIPMENT
1 chinois (fine sieve)
1 flexible spatula
1 kitchen thermometer
1 immersion blender
1 piping bag fitted with a plain tip, ¾ in. (2 cm) diameter
1 pair of thin disposable gloves
1 dipping fork
1 baking sheet
1 sieve

Prepare the bittersweet chocolate ganache.

Chop the chocolate and melt it slowly in a bain-marie or in the microwave oven (on "defrost" or at 500 W maximum, stirring from time to time). Slit the half vanilla bean lengthwise and scrape the seeds out into the cream. Bring the cream and honey to a boil with the half vanilla bean. Strain through a chinois (fine sieve).

Gradually pour one third of the boiling cream over the melted chocolate. Using a flexible spatula, mix it in energetically, drawing small circles to create an elastic, shiny "kernel."

Incorporate the second third of the cream, using the same procedure. Repeat with the last third.

As soon as the ganache has cooled to 95°F–104°F (35°C–40°C), but no cooler, stir in the diced butter. Process with an immersion blender so that the mixture is smooth and thoroughly emulsified. Leave to set for 3 hours in the refrigerator.

Spoon it into a piping bag and pipe out balls. As soon as the texture is sufficiently hard, roll them with your hands to shape them. It's best to use thin disposable gloves for this.

Prepare the coating.

Temper the bittersweet chocolate using the method of your choice (see pp. 13–15). Pour the tempered chocolate into a large mixing bowl. Pour out a sufficient quantity of cocoa powder to cover a baking sheet.

Use a dipping fork to coat the truffles. Press down lightly with the tip of the fork to submerge the truffle completely in the tempered chocolate. Retrieve the truffle with the fork and dip it 3 or 4 times more. This will create suction so that the chocolate coating will not be too thick. Then scrape the excess chocolate off the bottom of the truffle so that the coating is not too thick.

Carefully place the truffle in the cocoa powder and roll it immediately to cover it. Leave the truffles to harden in the cocoa powder. When the truffles have set, place them in a sieve to remove any excess cocoa powder.

Chef's note

It's important not to let the ganache cool too much or its texture will become grainy.

Moist

Black Forest Cake

SERVES 6–8 · PREPARATION TIME: 2 HOURS · COOKING TIME: 10 MINUTES · CHILLING TIME: 1 HOUR

INGREDIENTS

Kirsch syrup
1 ¼ cups (300 ml) syrup from the jar of cherries (see below)
2 tablespoons plus 2 teaspoons (40 ml) kirsch

Chocolate sponge
Generous ¼ cup (1 oz./25 g) cake flour
3 tablespoons (⅔ oz./20 g) unsweetened cocoa powder
4 eggs: 2 whole, 2 separated
⅓ cup (2 ⅔ oz./75 g) granulated sugar
2 ½ tablespoons (1 oz./30 g) light brown sugar (*cassonade*)

Light kirsch-flavored cream
1 sheet (2 g) gelatin
1 vanilla bean
¾ cup (200 ml) full-fat whipping cream
1 heaped tablespoon (15 g) sugar
1 tablespoon plus 1 teaspoon (20 ml) kirsch
1 jar of griottes cherries, net weight 7 oz. (200 g)

Bittersweet chocolate ganache glaze
5 ½ oz. (150 g) bittersweet chocolate, 60 percent cocoa
1 cup (250 ml) full-fat whipping cream
Scant 3 tablespoons (60 g) honey
4 tablespoons (2 ¼ oz./60 g) butter, diced

To decorate
Chocolate tuiles or other decorations
Confectioners' sugar (optional)

EQUIPMENT
1 colander
1 sieve
1 whisk
1 large baking sheet
1 pastry ring, 6 ½ in. (16 cm) diameter
1 cake cooling rack
1 pastry brush
1 flexible spatula

Prepare the kirsch syrup.
Thirty minutes before you need them, drain the cherries in a colander placed over a bowl. Add the kirsch to the syrup from the jar.

Prepare the chocolate sponge.
Preheat the oven to 350°F (180°C). Sift the flour and cocoa together and set aside.

In a mixing bowl, whisk the 2 whole eggs with 2 egg yolks and the granulated sugar until pale and thick. Whisk the 2 egg whites with the light brown sugar. Gradually combine the two mixtures. Pour in the sifted dry ingredients and fold in until just combined. Pour the batter onto a large baking sheet and bake for 7 to 8 minutes. The texture should be spongy and the tip of a knife should come out dry. Leave to cool.

Prepare the light kirsch-flavored cream.
Soften the gelatin in a bowl of very cold water. Slit the vanilla bean lengthwise and scrape out the seeds with the tip of a knife. Wring the water out of the gelatin sheets. Heat 3 tablespoons of whipping cream in a saucepan to dissolve the gelatin. Whisk the rest of the whipping cream with the sugar and vanilla seeds. Just before the cream reaches a Chantilly texture, fold in the cream and gelatin mixture as well as the kirsch. Continue whisking until you have a light Chantilly cream texture.

Use the pastry ring to cut out three disks of chocolate sponge. Place the first disk on a cake rack and with a pastry brush moisten it with the kirsch syrup. Use a spatula to spread out half the kirsch-flavored cream and arrange half the cherries evenly on this layer. Place the second disk above this and repeat the procedure. Top with the third disk of chocolate sponge and chill.

Prepare the bittersweet chocolate ganache glaze (see p. 21) using the proportions given here.
Pour the ganache glaze over the cake so that it is completely glazed. Chill for 1 hour.

Arrange the chocolate tuiles or other decorations on the ganache so that the cake is entirely covered. Dust lightly with confectioners' sugar, if desired.

Chocolate–Vanilla Marble Loaf

SERVES 6–8 · PREPARATION TIME: 20 MINUTES · COOKING TIME: 50–60 MINUTES

INGREDIENTS

Vanilla batter

8 egg yolks
1 cup plus 2 tablespoons (7 ¾ oz./220 g) granulated sugar
½ cup (120 ml) whipping cream
1 vanilla bean
1 cup plus generous ¾ cup (5 ¾ oz./165 g) cake flour
¾ teaspoon (3 g) baking powder
4 ½ tablespoons (2 ⅓ oz./65 g) butter, melted and cooled

Chocolate batter

2 ½ oz. (70 g) bittersweet chocolate, 70 percent cocoa
4 egg yolks
Scant ⅔ cup (4 ¼ oz./120 g) sugar
Scant ⅓ cup (70 ml) whipping cream
Scant cup (2 ¾ oz./80 g) cake flour
2 teaspoons (5 g) unsweetened cocoa powder
½ teaspoon (2 g) baking powder
1 tablespoon plus 1 teaspoon (20 ml) grape-seed oil

A little melted butter to dip the spatula (optional)

EQUIPMENT

1 whisk or handheld electric beater
1 sieve
1 loaf pan, 3 × 12 × 3 in. (8 × 30 × 8 cm)
Parchment paper
2 piping bags
1 flexible spatula
Cake cooling rack

Prepare the vanilla batter.

In a mixing bowl, combine the egg yolks with the sugar. Add the cream. Slit the vanilla bean lengthwise and scrape out the seeds into the mixture. Sift in the flour and baking powder and incorporate them into the batter, then stir in the melted butter. Set aside.

Prepare the chocolate batter.

Chop the chocolate and melt it slowly in a bain-marie or in the microwave oven (on "defrost" or at 500 W maximum, stirring from time to time).

In a mixing bowl, combine the egg yolks with the sugar, then stir in the cream. Sift the flour, cocoa powder, and baking powder together into the mixture and stir in. Then stir in the melted chocolate and grape-seed oil until just blended.

Preheat the oven to 300°F (150°C). Line the loaf pan with parchment paper. Spoon the vanilla batter and chocolate batter alternately into the loaf pan to create a marbled pattern. Alternatively, use two piping bags to pipe out the batters. Pipe out one third of the vanilla batter over the bottom of the pan, then pipe out half of the chocolate batter lengthwise through the center. Cover this with one third of the vanilla batter and pipe out the remaining half of the chocolate batter lengthwise through the center. Cover it with the remaining vanilla batter. Dip a spatula into a little melted butter and run it lengthwise along the batter, making an incision about ½ in. (1–2 cm) deep so that the cake rises nicely.

Bake for 50 minutes to 1 hour, until the tip of a knife or cake tester comes out clean. Turn the cake out onto a cake rack and leave it for about 10 minutes on its side so that it retains its shape.

Chocolate Éclairs

SERVES 6–8 · PREPARATION TIME: 1 HOUR · COOKING TIME: 20 MINUTES · CHILLING TIME: 1 HOUR

INGREDIENTS

1 quantity chocolate pastry cream (see p. 30)

Choux pastry
Scant ¼ cup (50 ml) water
Scant ¼ cup (60 ml) whole milk
1 pinch table salt
1 pinch sugar
2 tablespoons plus 2 teaspoons (1 ½ oz./40 g) butter
⅔ cup (2 oz./60 g) cake flour
2 eggs

Soft chocolate glaze
4 ½ oz. (130 g) bittersweet chocolate, 70 percent cocoa
½ cup minus 1 ½ tablespoons (100 ml) whipping cream

EQUIPMENT
1 sieve
2 piping bags, 1 fitted with a large plain tip
  and 1 with a small plain tip
Baking sheets lined with food-safe acetate
  or parchment paper
1 flexible spatula
1 immersion blender
1 kitchen thermometer

Prepare the chocolate pastry cream (see p. 30). Set aside in the refrigerator.

Prepare the choux pastry.
Preheat the oven to 480°F (250°C).

In a saucepan, bring the water, milk, salt, sugar, and butter to a boil. Sift the flour into the liquid. The important step now is to dry it out: stir energetically until the moisture has evaporated. Remove from the heat and mix in the eggs, one by one. Stir thoroughly each time. When the batter is ready it should have a satin finish, like paint. If it is matte it is already too hard; if it is shiny it is too wet.

Spoon the batter into a piping bag fitted with a large plain tip and pipe out the pastry onto lined baking sheets in éclair shapes, or pipe out three small puff pastries side by side to form a line as long as a traditional éclair. Place in the oven and immediately switch off the heat. As soon as the dough begins to puff up and color, turn the heat back on to 350°F (180°C) and leave the pastries to dry out slowly for about 10 minutes.

Prepare the soft chocolate glaze.
Chop the chocolate and melt it slowly in a bain-marie or in the microwave oven (on "defrost" or at 500 W maximum, stirring from time to time). In a saucepan, bring the whipping cream to a boil. Slowly pour one third of the hot cream over the melted chocolate. Using a flexible spatula, mix in energetically, drawing small circles to create an elastic, shiny "kernel." Incorporate the second third of the liquid, using the same procedure. Repeat with the last third. Blend for a few seconds using an immersion blender, making sure you do not incorporate any air bubbles. Set aside in the refrigerator.

Assemble the éclairs.
Spoon the pastry cream into a piping bag fitted with a small plain tip and pipe it into the éclairs. Heat the glaze just slightly—it should be at a temperature of 82°F–86°F (28°C–30°C)—and glaze the rounded tops of the éclairs. Refrigerate until you serve them.

Chef's note
If you wish, you may freeze your choux pastry either raw or baked. If the éclairs are already baked, defrost them in the oven at 375°F–400°F (190°C–200°C) to restore their crispness.

Chocolate Soufflé

SERVES 6 · PREPARATION TIME: 20 MINUTES · COOKING TIME: 10–12 MINUTES · CHILLING TIME: 30 MINUTES

INGREDIENTS
A little butter, melted, to grease the soufflé molds
5 ½ oz. (150 g) bittersweet chocolate, 70 percent cocoa
4 eggs, separated
½ cup (3 ½ oz./100 g) sugar, plus a little extra for sprinkling the molds
1 heaped teaspoon unsweetened cocoa powder
1 heaped teaspoon cornstarch
¾ cup (200 ml) whipping cream

EQUIPMENT
1 pastry brush
6 individual soufflé molds or ramekins
1 whisk
1 sieve
1 flexible spatula

Using a pastry brush, carefully butter the molds with butter. Then sprinkle them all over with sugar, turning them upside down to remove the excess. Set aside in the refrigerator.

Chop the chocolate and melt it slowly in a bain-marie or in the microwave oven (on "defrost" or at 500 W maximum, stirring from time to time).

Slowly start whisking the egg whites, gradually adding the sugar. Continue until they form soft peaks.

Sift the cocoa powder and cornstarch together. Pour the cold cream into a saucepan and add the sifted ingredients. Bring to a boil, stirring constantly so that the liquid does not stick. When it simmers and starts to thicken, remove from the heat and slowly pour one third over the melted chocolate. Using a flexible spatula, mix it in energetically, drawing small circles to create an elastic, shiny "kernel." Incorporate the second third of the liquid, using the same procedure. Repeat with the last third.

Add the egg yolks, whisking energetically until the texture is smooth and shiny. Carefully fold in one third of the whisked egg whites with a spatula. When the consistency has been lightened, carefully fold in the remaining egg whites.

Fill the molds up to the top, cleaning the rim so that the batter does not stick to it and so that the soufflés can rise straight up. Chill until they are to be baked.

About 30 minutes before serving the dessert, preheat the oven to 425°F (210°C–220°C).

Remove the soufflés from the refrigerator and bake for about 10 to 12 minutes, until well risen with a nicely done crust. Serve immediately.

Cactus-Shaped Churros with Ginger-Chocolate Sauce

SERVES 6–8 · PREPARATION TIME: 1 HOUR · COOKING TIME: 10 MINUTES · FREEZING TIME: 3 HOURS

INGREDIENTS

Churros
¾ cup (185 ml) milk
Heaped ½ teaspoon (3 g) salt
1 teaspoon (4 g) sugar
5 tablespoons plus 1 teaspoon (2 ⅔ oz./75 g) butter
Generous ½ cup (1 ¾ oz./50 g) cake flour
3 eggs

Ginger–chocolate sauce
3 ¾ oz. (110 g) milk chocolate, 40 percent cocoa
1 cup minus 1 tablespoon (235 ml) whipping cream
2 teaspoons (½ oz./15 g) glucose syrup
1 small piece of ginger root, just over 1 in. (3 cm)
Scant ⅔ cup (4 ¼ oz./120 g) sugar
2 tablespoons plus 2 teaspoons (1 ½ oz./40 g) butter

Flavored sugar
1 unwaxed lime
1 cup (7 oz./200 g) sugar

2 cups (500 ml) oil for frying

EQUIPMENT

1 piping bag fitted with a star-shaped tip
1 baking sheet lined with parchment paper
  or 1 silicone baking mat
1 blender or fine grater
1 flexible spatula
1 immersion blender
1 deep fry pot
1 kitchen thermometer

Prepare the churros.

Bring the milk, salt, sugar, and butter to a boil in a saucepan. Pour the flour into the mixture and stir for 1 minute over high heat to dry out the dough. Remove from the heat and incorporate the eggs, one by one, stirring well each time, until the dough is smooth and forms a soft ball.

Spoon the dough into a piping bag and pipe out small cactus shapes onto a lined baking sheet. Freeze for about 3 hours.

Prepare the ginger–chocolate sauce.

Chop the chocolate and melt it slowly in a bain-marie or in the microwave oven (on "defrost" or at 500 W maximum, stirring from time to time).

Bring the cream to a boil with the glucose syrup. Peel the ginger and extract the juice using a blender, or reduce it to a fine pulp with a grater.

Place one third of the sugar in a heavy-bottomed saucepan. Cook until it forms a light caramel. Add the next third of the sugar and stir. When this quantity has reached the same color—a light caramel—add the last third of the sugar, When the caramel is ready, incorporate the butter, being careful not to burn yourself, and then the heated cream and glucose mixture. Gradually pour one third of the mixture over the melted chocolate. Using a flexible spatula, mix it in energetically, drawing small circles to create an elastic, shiny "kernel." Incorporate the second third of the liquid, using the same procedure. Repeat with the last third. Process for a few seconds using an immersion blender so that the mixture is smooth and perfectly emulsified, and then stir in the ginger juice or pulp.

Prepare the flavored sugar.

Grate the lime zest using a fine grater, or chop it very finely. Combine it thoroughly with the sugar.

Heat the oil to 356°F (180°C) in a deep pot or deep fryer. Carefully drop in two to three frozen churros at a time and fry them until a nice golden color.

Drain them on paper towel and sprinkle them with the flavored sugar. Serve with the warm ginger–chocolate sauce.

Chocolate Waffles

SERVES 6–8 · PREPARATION TIME: 45–50 MINUTES · COOKING TIME: 4 MINUTES PER BATCH OF WAFFLES

INGREDIENTS

Milk chocolate and maple syrup sauce
1 cup (10 ½ oz./300 g) maple syrup
Scant ⅔ cup (150 ml) whipping cream
3 ½ oz. (100 g) milk chocolate, 40 percent cocoa

Chocolate waffle batter
1 generous cup (110 g) all-purpose flour
1 ¾ oz. (50 g) bittersweet chocolate, 70 percent cocoa
½ cup (125 ml) whole milk
1 tablespoon plus 1 teaspoon (20 ml) vanilla extract
¼ cup (1 ¾ oz./50 g) granulated sugar

1 stick plus 1 teaspoon (4 ⅔ oz./130 g) butter
Scant ½ teaspoon (2 g) table salt
3 egg whites

Vanilla ice cream, to serve

EQUIPMENT
1 kitchen thermometer
1 flexible spatula
1 sieve
1 whisk
1 waffle maker

Prepare the chocolate and maple syrup sauce.
Heat the maple syrup in a saucepan to 250°F (120°C). While it is cooking, slightly warm the cream. When the maple syrup has reached the right temperature, stir in the cream and bring back to a boil.

Chop the chocolate and melt it gently in a bain-marie or in the microwave oven (on "defrost" or at 500 W maximum, stirring from time to time).

Gradually pour one third of the boiling liquid over the melted chocolate. Using a flexible spatula, mix it in energetically, drawing small circles to create an elastic, shiny "kernel."

Incorporate the second third of the liquid, using the same procedure. Repeat with the last third.

Prepare the chocolate waffle batter.
Sift the flour into a mixing bowl. Chop the chocolate and melt it slowly in a bain-marie or in the microwave oven (on "defrost" or at 500 W maximum, stirring from time to time). In a saucepan,

bring the milk to a boil, then add the vanilla extract, sugar, butter, and salt. Incorporate the chocolate, third by third, into the hot liquid, stirring energetically each time. Then pour the mixture into the sifted flour and combine. Whisk the egg whites to soft peaks and fold them in carefully.

Heat the waffle maker. When it is hot, spoon the batter over the grids and cook for about 4 minutes.

Place the waffles on plates and serve with a scoop of vanilla ice cream, drizzled with chocolate–maple syrup sauce.

Chef's notes
You can prepare the waffles ahead of time. Sprinkle them with confectioners' sugar for added crunch, and reheat them in the oven on "broil."

Bringing the maple syrup to 250°F (120°C) brings out its aromas and makes it more syrupy. The cream must be warmed separately.

Chocolate-Pistachio Loaf with Almond-Anise Streusel

SERVES 6 · PREPARATION TIME: 45 MINUTES · COOKING TIME: 1 HOUR 10 MINUTES

INGREDIENTS

Almond and anise streusel
1 tablespoon plus 2 ½ teaspoons (⅓ oz./10 g) cake flour
1 tablespoon plus 1 scant tablespoon (⅓ oz./10 g)
   ground blanched almonds
2 ½ teaspoons (10 g) light brown sugar (*cassonade*)
Small pinch salt
1 pinch ground green anise
2 teaspoons (⅓ oz./10 g) butter, well chilled

Pistachio loaf cake
1 tablespoon (½ oz./15 g) butter
⅓ cup (2 ⅔ oz./75 g) granulated sugar
1 egg
1 pinch table salt
2 tablespoons plus 1 teaspoon (35 ml) whipping cream
⅔ cup (2 oz./60 g) cake flour
¼ teaspoon (1 g) baking powder
1 oz. (30 g) pistachio paste (see p. 188, or buy from
   specialty stores or online)

Light chocolate cake
1 tablespoon plus 1 teaspoon (⅔ oz./20 g) butter
⅓ cup (1 oz./30 g) cake flour
½ teaspoon (2 g) baking powder
1 tablespoon (¼ oz./8 g) unsweetened cocoa powder
1 egg
¼ cup (1 ¾ oz./50 g) granulated sugar
¼ cup (⅔ oz./20 g) ground blanched almonds
1 ¼ oz. (35 g) bittersweet chocolate, 60 or 70 percent cocoa
2 tablespoons (30 ml) whipping cream
1 egg white

A few candied cherries, such as Amarena cherries

EQUIPMENT
1 sieve
1 baking sheet or 1 silicone baking mat
1 whisk or handheld electric beater
1 loaf pan, 10 in. (25 cm)
Parchment paper

Prepare the almond and anise streusel.
Follow the recipe on p. 187 (but use the reduced quantities indicated above), adding the pinch of ground green anise along with the dry ingredients.

Prepare the pistachio loaf cake.
Heat the butter in a saucepan until it is just melted. In a mixing bowl, combine the sugar with the egg, salt, and whipping cream until the texture is liquid. Sift the flour with the baking powder and stir it into the mixture until it forms a smooth batter.

Lightly soften the pistachio paste in the microwave oven and mix a little of the batter into it. When this mixture is quite smooth, mix it into the remaining batter with the melted butter.

Prepare the light chocolate cake.
Heat the butter in a saucepan until it is just melted.

Sift the flour with the baking powder and cocoa powder and set aside. Whisk the egg with the sugar until thick and pale. Add the ground almonds and the other, sifted dry ingredients. Stir them in until just mixed. Set aside at room temperature.

Chop the chocolate and melt it slowly in a bain-marie or in the microwave oven (on "defrost" or at 500 W maximum, stirring from time to time).

Heat the whipping cream and combine it with the melted chocolate. Add the chocolate–cream mixture to the batter, then stir in the melted butter. Whisk the egg white and fold it in carefully.

Preheat the oven to 300°F (150°C). Line the loaf pan with parchment paper. Pour the pistachio batter into the bottom of the pan. Scatter a few candied cherries over the batter, taking care that they do not touch the sides of the pan. Pour in the

chocolate batter, and then sprinkle the baked streusel over it.

Bake for about 1 hour. Check for doneness with the tip of a knife. The cake is ready when it comes out dry.

Chef's note
This cake will develop its aromas overnight. Wrap it in plastic wrap so that it keeps well. If you like a crisp crust, wrap the cake once it has cooled down. If you prefer it soft, wrap it while it is still warm.

Chocolate-Banana Loaf Cake with Rum-Soaked Raisins

**SERVES 6 · PREPARATION TIME: 20 MINUTES
COOKING TIME: 40–50 MINUTES · CHILLING TIME: OVERNIGHT**

INGREDIENTS
Rum-soaked raisins
Generous ⅓ cup (2 ¼ oz./60 g) golden raisins
3 tablespoons plus 1 teaspoon (50 ml) white rum
Scant tablespoon water

Cake batter
7 tablespoons (3 ½ oz./100 g) butter
2 ¾ oz. (80 g) bittersweet chocolate, 60 percent cocoa
3 ½ tablespoons (1 ½ oz./40 g) granulated sugar
2 lightly packed tablespoons (⅔ oz./20 g) muscovado,
  light brown sugar (*cassonade*), or other brown sugar
1 egg yolk
3 eggs
2 (7 oz./200 g) very ripe, almost black bananas, puréed
Scant ½ cup (1 ½ oz./40 g) ground hazelnuts

1 ½ oz. (40 g) cocoa nibs
Generous ½ cup (1 ¾ oz./50 g) cake flour
1 teaspoon (4 g) baking powder
5 ½ oz. (150 g) milk chocolate, 40 percent cocoa

A little brown rum
A little grated nutmeg

EQUIPMENT
1 food processor fitted with a blade attachment
1 loaf pan, 10 in. (25 cm)
Parchment paper
Plastic wrap

A day ahead.
Rinse the golden raisins under boiling water and plump them up by simmering over low heat in the white rum and water until the liquid has been completely absorbed.

Prepare the cake batter.
Place the butter in a saucepan over low heat until just melted. Chop the chocolate and melt it slowly in a bain-marie or in the microwave oven (on "defrost" or at 500 W maximum, stirring from time to time). Pour the melted butter over the chocolate and then pour the mixture into the bowl of a food processor. Add the granulated and muscovado sugar. Process until smooth, then add the egg yolk and process again. Add the eggs, one by one, combining each time—the batter must remain smooth while you prepare it. Add the puréed bananas. Add the ground hazelnuts, cocoa nibs, flour, and baking powder and process again until just combined.

Chill for 15 minutes to allow the batter to harden. Preheat the oven to 350°F (180°C).

While the batter is chilling, chop the milk chocolate. Take the batter out of the refrigerator and stir in the rum-flavored raisins and chopped milk chocolate. Line a loaf pan with parchment paper; alternatively, butter it and dust it with flour, rapping it upside down to remove any excess. Pour the batter into a prepared pan. Bake for about 45 minutes, until it is well risen.

When you remove the cake from the oven, moisten it with the brown rum and grate a little nutmeg over the top. While it is still hot, cover it tightly in plastic wrap. All the rum flavors will penetrate the cake and none of the taste or the alcohol will evaporate. Leave to chill overnight in the refrigerator.

Chocolate *Financiers* with Citrus Streusel and Candied Orange Peel

SERVES 6–8 · PREPARATION TIME: 30 MINUTES · CHILLING TIME: 2–3 HOURS · COOKING TIME: 30 MINUTES

INGREDIENTS

Chocolate *financiers*
2 ¼ cups (6 ¾ oz./190 g) ground blanched almonds
1 generous cup (5 ½ oz./150 g) confectioners' sugar
1 tablespoon (⅓ oz./10 g) cornstarch
1 ½ tablespoons (⅓ oz./10 g) unsweetened cocoa powder
9 egg whites
⅓ cup (75 ml) whipping cream
1 ¾ oz. (50 g) bittersweet chocolate, 60 percent cocoa

Citrus-flavored almond streusel
Generous ½ cup (1 ¾ oz./50 g) cake flour
Generous ½ cup (1 ¾ oz./50 g) ground blanched almonds
4 tablespoons (1 ¾ oz./50 g) light brown sugar (*cassonade*)

Generous pinch (3 g) fleur de sel or salt
Zest of ½ unwaxed orange
Zest of ½ unwaxed lemon
3 tablespoons plus 1 teaspoon (1 ¾ oz./50 g) butter

(Alternatively, the streusel can be replaced by 1 packet
   shortbread cookies, crushed)

8 ½ oz. (240 g) diced candied orange peel

EQUIPMENT
1 flexible spatula
1 baking sheet with *financier* molds

Prepare the chocolate *financiers*.
Combine the ground almonds, confectioners' sugar, cornstarch, and cocoa powder in a mixing bowl. Lightly beat the egg whites with a fork to liquefy them. Incorporate the egg whites and whipping cream into the dry ingredients. Set the batter aside.

Chop the chocolate and melt it slowly in a bain-marie or in the microwave oven (on "defrost" or at 500 W maximum, stirring from time to time).

Pour a little of the batter over the melted chocolate, stirring energetically with a flexible spatula to combine. Then carefully fold this mixture back into the remaining batter. Chill for at least 2 to 3 hours. This is an important stage in the recipe, as it will allow the *financiers* to rise well when baked.

Prepare the citrus-flavored almond streusel.
Follow the recipe on p. 187, using the ingredients and quantities indicated above, adding the citrus zests with the dry ingredients.

Prepare the *financiers* for baking.
Preheat the oven to 350°F (180°C).

Pour the chocolate batter into the molds and sprinkle with diced candied orange and baked streusel crumbs or crushed cookies. Total baking time is 15 to 20 minutes. However, to ensure that the streusel and diced orange peel stay at the top of these little cakes, you may bake them in two stages. Bake the *financier* batter for 4 minutes, then sprinkle with the two topping ingredients, and return to the oven for about 10 minutes.

Brownies

SERVES 8 · PREPARATION TIME: 10 MINUTES · COOKING TIME: 20 MINUTES

INGREDIENTS

3 eggs
Scant ⅔ cup (4 ¼ oz./120 g) granulated sugar
Scant ⅔ cup (4 ¼ oz./120 g) light brown sugar (*cassonade*)
3 ¼ oz. (90 g) bittersweet chocolate, 60 percent cocoa
1 ½ sticks (6 oz./170 g) butter
7 tablespoons (1 ½ oz./40 g) cake flour
1 ½ tablespoons (10 g) unsweetened cocoa powder
A handful of walnuts and/or pecan nuts, macadamia nuts,
  or Valrhona chocolate pearls, chopped chocolate,
  or chocolate chips

EQUIPMENT

1 sieve
1 brownie pan, 8 in. (20 cm) square, or 1 tart pan, 8 in.
  (20 cm) diameter, lined with parchment paper

Preheat the oven to 325°F (160°C).

In a mixing bowl, combine the eggs with the two types of sugar, being careful to ensure that the mixture does not bubble.

Chop the chocolate with the butter and melt slowly in a bain-marie or in the microwave oven (on "defrost" or at 500 W maximum, stirring from time to time).

Stir the melted chocolate and butter into the egg and sugar mixture.

Sift in the flour and cocoa together and stir in until just mixed.

Pour the batter into the lined brownie pan or tart pan. Sprinkle with nuts of your choice, or chocolate pearls, or any of the alternatives. Bake for about 20 minutes. The brownies should be softly cooked, almost molten.

Leave to cool in the pan. Serve when cooled.

Chef's notes

To make it easier to cut up the brownies, place the pan in the freezer for a few minutes.

These brownies are even more delicious with a scoop of vanilla ice cream, salted butter caramel sauce, or a little Chantilly cream.

Cupcakes

MAKES 18 CUPCAKES · PREPARATION TIME: 40 MINUTES
COOKING TIME: 15 MINUTES · CHILLING TIME: 3 HOURS

INGREDIENTS

Chocolate cupcake batter
5 ½ tablespoons (2 ¾ oz./80 g) butter
1 ¾ oz. (50 g) bittersweet chocolate, 70 percent cocoa
1 cup minus 1 tablespoon (2 ⅔ oz./75 g) ground
  blanched almonds
1 ⅓ cups (4 ¼ oz./120 g) cake flour
3 ½ tablespoons (1 oz./25 g) unsweetened cocoa powder
2 level teaspoons (8 g) baking powder
5 eggs
3 ½ tablespoons (2 ⅔ oz./75 g) honey
⅔ cup (4 1/2 oz./125 g) sugar
½ cup (120 ml) whipping cream

Or Plain cupcake batter (to be flavored)
5 ½ tablespoons (2 ¾ oz./80 g) butter
1 ⅔ cups (11 oz./310 g) granulated sugar
5 eggs
1 pinch table salt
Generous ½ cup (135 ml) whipping cream
2 ⅔ cups (8 ½ oz./240 g) cake flour
1 level teaspoon (4 g) baking powder
Your choice of flavoring, such as spices or citrus zest

Whipped ganache, to be flavored and/or colored
5 ⅔ oz. (160 g) white chocolate, 35 percent cocoa
Whipping cream, divided as follows: ½ cup minus
  1 tablespoon (110 ml) and 1 cup plus 1 tablespoon (270 ml)
Your choice of flavoring, such as citrus zest, spices,
  essential oils, etc.

Or Whipped bittersweet chocolate ganache
Whipping cream, divided as follows: ½ cup minus
  1 tablespoon (110 ml) and 1 cup minus 3 tablespoons
  (200 ml)
3 ¼ oz. (90 g) bittersweet chocolate, 70 percent cocoa

Decorations
Crystallized flowers, pearls, chocolate sprinkles, fruit, etc.

EQUIPMENT
1 sieve
1 whisk
1 piping bag
Plain and star-shaped piping tips
1 baking sheet with 18 cupcake liners
1 flexible spatula

Prepare the chocolate cupcakes.

Preheat the oven to 325°F (160°C). Melt the butter and set it aside. Chop the chocolate and melt it slowly in a bain-marie or in the microwave oven (on "defrost" or at 500 W maximum, stirring from time to time). Stir in the melted butter. Sift the almonds, flour, cocoa, and baking powder ingredients together. Whisk the eggs, honey, and sugar together until thick. Stir in the dry ingredients. Then stir in the whipping cream, and lastly, the melted chocolate and butter. Spoon the batter into a piping bag and pipe it out into the cups to two thirds of their height. Bake for about 15 minutes, until the tip of a knife or cake tester comes out dry.

Prepare the cupcake batter with your choice of flavoring.

Preheat the oven to 325°F (160°C). Melt the butter and set it aside. Combine the sugar, eggs, salt, and cream. Sift the flour with the baking powder and stir it into the egg mixture. Stir in the melted butter and your flavoring. Spoon the batter into a piping bag and pipe it out into the cups to two thirds of their height. Bake for about 15 minutes, until a nice golden color and the tip of a knife or cake tester comes out dry.

Make the whipped ganache (to be flavored or colored).

Chop the white chocolate and melt it slowly in a bain-marie or in the microwave oven (on "defrost" or at 500 W maximum, stirring from time to time). Bring the scant ½ cup (110 ml) cream to a boil. Gradually pour one third of the boiling cream over the melted chocolate. Using a flexible spatula, mix it in energetically, drawing small circles to create an elastic, shiny "kernel." Incorporate the second third of the cream, using the same

procedure. Repeat with the last third. Stir the remaining cream (cold) into the ganache. Flavor or color it as you wish. Leave to set for at least 3 hours in the refrigerator, then whip it until the texture softens.

To prepare the whipped bittersweet chocolate ganache, use the same procedure.

Ice and decorate.
Pipe out a decorative rosette of whipped ganache over the cupcakes using a piping bag fitted with a star-shaped tip.

Decorate however you desire.

Gianduja-Topped Madeleines

MAKES ABOUT 20 MADELEINES · PREPARATION TIME: 15 MINUTES
CHILLING TIME: 3–4 HOURS · COOKING TIME: 10 MINUTES

INGREDIENTS

2 ¼ sticks (9 oz./250 g) butter, plus a little extra
   to grease the baking pan
5 eggs
½ teaspoon vanilla seeds or ground vanilla bean
1 ¼ cups (9 oz./250 g) sugar
2 teaspoons (15 g) honey
2 ¾ cups (9 oz./250 g) cake flour, plus a little extra
   for dusting the baking pan
2 level teaspoons (8 g) baking powder
7 oz. (200 g) gianduja

EQUIPMENT

1 kitchen thermometer
1 handheld electric beater or whisk
1 sieve
1 baking sheet with madeleine molds
2 piping bags, 1 fitted with a large plain tip and
   1 with a very small tip

Melt the butter and set aside to cool to 113°F (45°C). Beat the eggs, vanilla, sugar, and honey in a mixing bowl until all the ingredients are thoroughly mixed.

Sift in the flour and baking powder and fold in. Stir in the melted, cooled butter. Chill the batter for 3 to 4 hours.

Preheat the oven to 400°F (200°C).

Prepare the madeleine baking pan. Grease the molds and dust them lightly with flour, tapping the pan upside down to remove any excess flour.

Pipe out the madeleine batter into the pan using a large plain tip and bake for 8 to 10 minutes. They should peak in the center and be a nice golden color.

Melt the gianduja gently over a bain-marie or in the microwave oven (on "defrost" or at 500 W maximum, stirring from time to time.) When it has thickened a little, spoon it into the piping bag fitted with a very small tip.

Remove the madeleines from the oven and garnish with the gianduja. Leave to cool.

Chef's note

We strongly recommend chilling the batter for a few hours so that the madeleines rise nicely in the oven.

Hazelnut Praline Christmas Log

SERVES 6–8 · PREPARATION TIME: 1 HOUR · COOKING TIME: 7 MINUTES · CHILLING TIME: 3 HOURS

INGREDIENTS

Plain jelly-roll sponge
Generous ½ cup (1 ¾ oz./50 g) cake flour
2 eggs, whole
2 eggs, separated
Granulated sugar, divided as follows: scant ½ cup
  (2 ¾ oz./80 g) plus 2 ½ tablespoons (1 oz./30 g)

Whipped chocolate–hazelnut ganache
5 ½ oz. (150 g) milk chocolate, 40 percent cocoa
4 ¼ oz. (120 g) hazelnut praline
Whipping cream, divided as follows: ⅔ cup (160 ml)
  plus 1 ⅔ cups (400 ml)

7 oz. (200 g) chopped hazelnuts
Confectioners' sugar for dusting

EQUIPMENT
1 handheld electric beater or whisk
1 sieve
1 jelly (Swiss) roll pan, lined with parchment paper
1 flexible spatula
1 immersion blender

Prepare the jelly roll.

Sift the flour and set aside. Beat the 2 whole eggs and 2 egg yolks with the scant ½ cup (2 ¾ oz./80 g) sugar until the mixture is pale and thick. Whisk the 2 egg whites with the 2 ½ tablespoons (1 oz./30 g) sugar to soft peaks.

Carefully fold the whisked egg whites into the first mixture and pour in the sifted flour. Stir until just combined.

Spread the batter out onto the pan and bake for about 5–7 minutes. It should be only very lightly colored. When cooled, leave at room temperature.

Prepare the whipped chocolate–hazelnut ganache.

Chop the chocolate and melt it slowly in a bain-marie or in the microwave oven (on "defrost" or at 500 W maximum, stirring from time to time). Add the praline. Bring the ⅔ cup (160 ml) whipping cream to a boil. Gradually pour one third of the boiling cream over the melted chocolate and praline. Using a flexible spatula, mix it in energetically, drawing small circles to create an elastic, shiny "kernel." Incorporate the second third of the cream, using the same procedure. Repeat with the last third.

Stir in the remaining 1 ⅔ cups (400 ml) cold cream. Process with an immersion blender until the mixture is smooth and thoroughly emulsified. Chill for at least 3 hours, and then whip the ganache at medium speed until it is creamy. If you whip it any faster, it will lose its light, creamy texture and will become fatty.

Assemble the Christmas log.

Turn the jelly roll sponge out of the pan. Spread one third of the ganache over it and sprinkle with a few roughly chopped hazelnuts. Roll up the sponge and cover completely with the remaining whipped ganache. Decorate with the remaining chopped hazelnuts and dust with confectioners' sugar.

Milk Chocolate *Palets* with Caramel

SERVES 6–8 · PREPARATION TIME: 45 MINUTES · COOKING TIME: 9 MINUTES
COOLING TIME: 4 HOURS 30 MINUTES

INGREDIENTS
Caramel bonbon filling
3 ½ oz. (100 g) milk chocolate, 40 percent cocoa
Scant ¼ cup (50 ml) water
Granulated sugar divided as follows: 1 ¼ cups
  (8 ½ oz./240 g) plus scant ½ cup (2 ¾ oz./80 g)
⅔ cup (180 ml) whipping cream
2 ⅔ oz. (75 g) glucose syrup
2 pinches table salt
2 tablespoons (1 oz./30 g) butter, cubed

Sponge cake batter
1 ¾ oz. (50 g) milk chocolate, 40 percent cocoa

1 stick (4 ½ oz./125 g) butter
2 eggs
4 oz. (115 g) caramel filling (see below)
2 teaspoons (10 ml) whole milk
Scant ⅔ cup (2 ¼ oz./60 g) all-purpose flour

EQUIPMENT
1 pastry brush
1 kitchen thermometer
1 confectionery frame, 8 in. (20 cm) square brownie pan,
  or 4 confectionery rulers
6–8 silicone molds
1 piping bag

Prepare the caramel bonbon filling.
Chop the chocolate. In a saucepan, heat the water, then stir in the 1 ¼ cups (8 ½ oz./240 g) sugar. Dip a pastry brush in water and brush the sugar crystals away from the sides to dissolve all the sugar. Bring the syrup to a temperature of 350°F (180°C).

While it is heating, combine the cream, glucose syrup, salt, and scant ½ cup (2 ¾ oz./80 g) sugar in another saucepan and bring to a boil. When the water, and sugar mixture reaches the desired temperature of 350°F (180°C), carefully add the cubed butter. Stir briefly and then add the hot cream mixture and the chopped chocolate. The temperature of the mixture will be lowered. Stir continuously until the mixture reaches 250°F (120°C). Pour the caramel into the confectionery frame or prepared brownie pan. Leave to cool at room temperature for about 4 hours. Cut into 1 ¾ in. (2 cm) squares.

Prepare the sponge cake batter.
Chop the chocolate and melt it slowly in a bain-marie or in the microwave oven (on "defrost" or at 500 W maximum, stirring from time to time). In a mixing bowl, soften the butter.

Pour the melted chocolate over the softened butter and mix until the ingredients have combined smoothly. Add the eggs one by one, stirring each time and ensuring that the mixture remains smooth.

Slightly heat the milk. Take 4 oz. (115 g) of the cut-out caramels and melt them in the heated milk. Incorporate the milk–caramel mixture into the chocolate and egg mixture. Sift in the flour, and combine.

Assemble the *palets*.
Preheat the oven to 350°F (180°C). Place a caramel bonbon in each mold. Spoon the caramel sponge cake batter into a piping bag and pipe it over the bonbon. Bake for about 9 minutes, until the tip of a knife comes out dry. Remove from the oven and leave to cool for 30 minutes before turning out of the molds.

Klemanga

SERVES 6–8 · PREPARATION TIME: 1 HOUR 20 MINUTES
COOKING TIME: 10 MINUTES · TOTAL FREEZING TIME: 4 HOURS · DEFROSTING TIME: 6 HOURS

INGREDIENTS

Soft coconut sponge
6 egg whites, divided (2 plus 4)
⅔ cup (2 oz./55 g) finely ground coconut
Generous ¼ cup (1 oz./25 g) cake flour
Scant ½ cup (2 oz./55 g) confectioners' sugar
1 tablespoon (15 ml) whipping cream
⅓ cup (2 ½ oz./70 g) granulated sugar

Mango–passion fruit coulis
¾ sheet (1.5 g) gelatin
5 ¾ oz. (165 g) fresh mango, peeled and pit removed
  (net weight)
2 ⅔ oz. (85 g) mango pulp, store-bought or homemade,
  with 10 percent sugar
1 ¾ oz. (50 g) passion fruit pulp (if using fresh passion fruit,
  it's best to strain it)
A little granulated sugar (optional)

Chocolate Chantilly mousse
4 ⅔ oz. (130 g) bittersweet chocolate, 70 percent cocoa
Whipping cream, divided as follows: ½ cup plus
  1 tablespoon (140 ml) and ⅓ cup (80 ml)

A little unsweetened cocoa powder for dusting

EQUIPMENT
1 whisk or handheld electric beater
1 jelly (Swiss) roll pan
1 pastry ring, 7–8 in. (18–20 cm) diameter
1 kitchen thermometer
1 silicone baking mat or a baking sheet lined
  with parchment paper
1 piping bag

Prepare the soft coconut sponge.
Preheat the oven to 350°F (180°C).

Lightly beat two egg whites. Combine the ground coconut, flour, and confectioners' sugar with the two egg whites and the whipping cream.

Whip the four remaining egg whites to soft peaks, gradually pouring in the granulated sugar as you whip. Carefully fold the beaten egg whites into the first mixture.

Spread out the batter in a lined jelly (Swiss) roll pan and bake for about 10 minutes.

Using the pastry ring as a cutter, cut out two disks of sponge.

Prepare the mango–passion fruit coulis.
Soften the gelatin in a bowl of cold water. Finely dice the mango flesh. Heat the mango and passion fruit pulps in a saucepan to 122°F (50°C), adding a little sugar if necessary. Wring the water out of the gelatin and dissolve it in the fruit pulp. Stir in the small mango cubes and set aside in the refrigerator.

Place the pastry ring on a silicone mat or lined baking sheet. Place one sponge disk at the base of the ring. Pour over the mango–passion fruit coulis, ensuring that you leave a little for the finishing. Top that with the second disk of sponge. Flatten lightly so that it is smooth. Freeze for 1 hour.

Prepare the chocolate Chantilly mousse.
Follow the instructions on p. 189, using the quantities given above.

Remove the dessert from the freezer. Spoon the Chantilly mousse into a piping bag and pipe out large balls of chocolate mousse on the top layer of sponge. Return to the freezer for an additional 3 hours.

Remove the pastry ring and place the dessert on a serving dish. Dust it with unsweetened cocoa powder. Slightly melt the mango–passion fruit coulis in the microwave oven, ensuring that you do not heat it, and decorate the dessert with it. This should not be eaten icy, so allow plenty of time— about 6 hours—for it to defrost in the refrigerator.

Mendiants

MAKES ABOUT 30 MENDIANTS · PREPARATION TIME: 45 MINUTES

INGREDIENTS

Your choice of dried fruit and nuts (dried apricots, almonds, walnuts, pistachios, etc.)
Either 10 ½ oz. (300 g) bittersweet chocolate, 70 percent cocoa
Or 10 ½ oz. (300 g) white chocolate, 35 percent cocoa
Or 10 ½ oz. (300 g) milk chocolate, 40 percent cocoa

EQUIPMENT

Baking sheets lined with parchment paper
1 kitchen thermometer
1 piping bag

Place your dried fruits and nuts in small bowls or ramekins, a separate bowl for each type.

Temper the chocolate.
Temper the chocolate using the technique of your choice (see pp. 13–15).

Fill a piping bag with the tempered chocolate and pipe identically sized chocolate drops, just under 1 in. (2 cm) in diameter, onto the prepared baking sheets. Rap the baking sheets lightly so that the drops spread out to form small disks (*palets*). Very quickly, top them with the dried fruit and nuts, and leave to set.

Chef's note
Do not pipe out too many drops of chocolate at a time so that you have time to place the dried fruit and nuts before the chocolate sets.

Orangettes

**SERVES 6–8 · PREPARATION TIME: 1 HOUR 30 MINUTES
COOKING TIME: 45 MINUTES · RESTING TIME: OVERNIGHT**

INGREDIENTS
3 large oranges, unwaxed
1 ¼ cups (9 oz./250 g) sugar
2 cups (500 ml) water
1 lb. (450 g) bittersweet chocolate, 70 percent cocoa

EQUIPMENT
1 colander
1 heavy-bottomed pot
1 wire rack
1 kitchen thermometer
1 dipping fork

A day ahead, prepare the orange peel.
Clean and brush the oranges under cold running water. Cut the peel into four quarters without making an incision into the flesh of the fruit. Carefully pull away the quarters of peel and place them in a large pot. Cover with cold water and bring to a boil. Leave to boil for 5 minutes. Drain, leave to cool, and repeat the procedure. Drain again and leave to cool in a colander.

In a heavy-bottomed pot, combine the sugar and water and bring to a boil. When the syrup begins to boil, drop the orange skins in. When it comes back to a boil, leave it to simmer for 5 minutes. Remove from the heat and leave the syrup with the orange peel to cool down again completely. Bring to a boil again twice, leaving the syrup to simmer 5 minutes each time and allowing it to cool down completely each time. The candied peel should be transparent after these three steps.

When the syrup and peel have finally cooled down, cut the peel into thin strips about ¼ in. (5 mm) wide. Place them on a rack, ensuring that they do not overlap and leave them to dry out, uncovered, for at least 12 hours.

Temper the chocolate.
Temper the chocolate using the technique of your choice (see pp. 13–15).

Use a dipping fork to coat the orange peel (see p. 18). Dip the strips of candied peel one by one in the tempered bittersweet chocolate. Leave to harden before serving.

Chef's note
If you prefer, you can find strips of candied orange peel ready to be coated at gourmet grocery stores.

Chocolate-Pecan Ladyfingers

SERVES 8 · PREPARATION TIME: 35–40 MINUTES · CHILLING TIME: 4 HOURS · COOKING TIME: 25 MINUTES

INGREDIENTS

Bittersweet chocolate ganache
4 ⅔ oz. (130 g) bittersweet chocolate, 70 percent cocoa
Generous ⅓ cup (90 ml) whipping cream
1 ½ tablespoons (1 oz./30 g) honey
3 tablespoons plus 1 teaspoon (1 ¾ oz./50 g) butter

Sponge layer
3 eggs, separated
4 lightly packed tablespoons plus 1 teaspoon (1 ⅔ oz./45 g)
  muscovado or brown sugar
2 slightly heaped tablespoons (1 ⅔ oz./45 g) chestnut or
  pine honey
Granulated sugar, divided as follows: scant ¼ cup
  (1 ⅔ oz./45 g) plus ⅓ cup (2 ½ oz./70 g)

3 ¼ oz. (90 g) bittersweet chocolate, 70 percent cocoa
1 ⅓ sticks (5 ½ oz./150 g) butter, softened
7 tablespoons (1 ½ oz./40 g) cake flour
2 ½ oz. (70 g) chopped pecan nuts
2 ½ oz. (70 g) chopped cashew nuts
White sesame seeds for sprinkling

EQUIPMENT
1 flexible spatula
1 kitchen thermometer
1 immersion blender
1 whisk or handheld electric beater
1 baking sheet lined with parchment paper
  or 1 silicone baking mat
1 piping bag

Prepare the ganache 3 to 4 hours ahead of time.
Make the ganache following the instructions on p. 21, but using the quantities given above, until you obtain a perfect emulsion, then chill for 3 to 4 hours.

Prepare the sponge layer.
Preheat the oven to 325°F (160°C).

In a large mixing bowl, combine the egg yolks, muscovado sugar, honey, and scant ¼ cup (1 ⅔ oz./45 g) sugar until the ingredients are just mixed. Set aside.

Chop the chocolate and melt it slowly in a bain-marie or in the microwave oven (on "defrost" or at 500 W maximum, stirring from time to time). Add the softened butter to the melted chocolate.

Whip the egg whites, gradually pouring in the ⅓ cup (2 ½ oz./70 g) sugar until the whites are shiny and stiff.

Fold the chocolate–butter mixture into the egg yolk and sugar mixture. Stir in the flour and the chopped nuts. Then carefully fold in the whipped egg whites.

Spread out the batter on a lined baking sheet to a thickness of about ⅔ in. (1.5 cm) and sprinkle with sesame seeds. Bake for about 25 minutes, until the tip of a knife inserted into the cake comes out dry. Remove from the oven and leave to rest for 5 minutes. Then turn it out onto a sheet of parchment paper. Place in the freezer for a few minutes and then cut out into finger shapes, 3 × ¾ in. (8 × 2 cm).

Once the fingers have cooled, pipe a strip of ganache along each one.

Chef's note
Hardening the sponge in the freezer makes it easy to cut it out into finger shapes.

Rochers ("Rock" Cookies)

MAKES ABOUT 1 LB. (500 G) OF *ROCHERS* · PREPARATION TIME: 50 MINUTES · SETTING TIME: 3 HOURS

INGREDIENTS

3 ½ oz. (100 g) milk chocolate, 40 percent cocoa
9 oz. (250 g) praline
⅓ oz. (10 g) crumbled *crêpes dentelles* (an extremely
  friable, fine wafer-like cookie, a Breton specialty)

Coating

3 ½ oz. (100 g) chopped almonds
1 lb. (500 g) bittersweet chocolate, 60 percent cocoa,
  or milk chocolate, 40 percent cocoa

EQUIPMENT

1 kitchen thermometer
1 baking sheet lined with parchment paper
1 handheld electric beater
1 piping bag
1 dipping fork

Chop the chocolate and melt it slowly in a bain-marie or in the microwave oven (on "defrost" or at 500 W maximum, stirring from time to time). Combine the melted chocolate with the praline. Place the mixing bowl in a larger bowl of ice water and cool the mixture down to 75°F (24°C), stirring constantly. Remove immediately from the water.

Stir in the crumbled *crêpes dentelles*, and pour the mixture onto a lined baking sheet. Leave to harden for a few hours.

When it has set, cut it into small pieces.

Place a few of the pieces in a mixing bowl and begin whisking with an electric beater. Gradually incorporate the remaining pieces until you have a smooth mixture.

Spoon it into a piping bag and pipe out small walnut-sized balls on to a lined baking sheet. Leave to harden before you coat them.

Roast the almonds and allow them to cool, then tip them onto a plate.

Temper the chocolate.
Temper the chocolate using the method of your choice (see pp. 13–15).

Dip the *rochers* in the tempered chocolate using a dipping fork, then roll them in the plate of chopped almonds. Leave to harden for a few minutes. Coat them once again in the tempered chocolate. If the chocolate has cooled, it is advisable to reheat it to 91°F (33°C) so that it doesn't crack.

Manhattan Cappuccino

SERVES 6–8 · PREPARATION TIME: 1 HOUR · CHILLING TIME: 3 HOURS MINIMUM

INGREDIENTS
2 packets rectangular dry butter cookies

Whipped milk chocolate–coffee ganache
3 ¾ oz. (110 g) milk chocolate, 40 percent cocoa
⅓ cup (80 ml) very strong espresso coffee
⅔ cup plus 2 teaspoons (190 ml) whipping cream

Coffee syrup
1 ¼ cups (300 ml) very strong espresso coffee
¼ cup (1 ¾ oz./50 g) granulated sugar

A few chopped, roasted almonds for decoration

EQUIPMENT
1 flexible spatula
1 silicone baking mat or sheets of food-safe acetate
1 handheld electric beater or whisk

Prepare the whipped milk chocolate–coffee ganache.

Chop the chocolate and melt it slowly in a bain-marie or in the microwave oven (on "defrost" or at 500 W maximum, stirring from time to time). Prepare the espresso coffee and gradually pour one third of the hot liquid over the melted chocolate. Using a flexible spatula, mix it in energetically, drawing small circles to create an elastic, shiny "kernel."

Incorporate the second third of the coffee, using the same procedure. Repeat with the last third. Mix in the cold whipping cream and leave to set in the refrigerator for at least 3 hours, but preferably overnight.

Prepare the coffee syrup.

Make some very strong espresso coffee and stir in the sugar. Leave to cool to room temperature before dipping the cookies.

Dip five cookies into the cooled coffee syrup and immediately place them side by side on a silicone baking mat or a sheet of food-safe acetate.

Remove the ganache from the refrigerator and whip it at medium speed until it reaches a creamy consistency.

Spread a thin layer of ganache over the cookies. Soak another five cookies in the coffee and repeat the operation twice more. Set aside a little whipped ganache to cover the edges.

Then construct the elements that will represent the buildings and high-rises with single and sandwiched pairs of cookies. Insert chopped toasted almonds into the gaps. Chill.

To serve, place the various components horizontally or vertically to evoke the Manhattan skyline.

Chef's note
This architecturally structured dessert is delicious served with chocolate sauce (see p. 33).

Gold-Topped *Palet* Dessert

SERVES 6 · PREPARATION TIME: 1 HOUR · COOKING TIME: 40 MINUTES
CHILLING TIME: OVERNIGHT PLUS 6 HOURS · FREEZING TIME: OVERNIGHT

INGREDIENTS

Ultra-shiny glaze
6 sheets (12 g) gelatin
Scant ½ cup (100 ml) water
Scant cup (6 oz./170 g) granulated sugar
⅔ cup (2 ⅔ oz./75 g) unsweetened cocoa powder
⅓ cup plus 2 teaspoons (90 ml) whipping cream

Chocolate cake layer
2 ½ oz. (70 g) bittersweet chocolate, 70 percent cocoa
1 stick (4 oz./120 g) butter, plus a little extra for the mold
1 ¾ cups (5 ⅔ oz./160 g) cake flour, plus a little extra
   for the mold
2 ½ teaspoons (10 g) baking powder
¼ cup (1 oz./30 g) unsweetened cocoa powder
6 eggs
Scant ⅓ cup (3 ½ oz./100 g) acacia honey
1 scant cup (6 oz./170 g) granulated sugar
1 cup plus 3 tablespoons (3 ½ oz./100 g) ground
   blanched almonds
⅔ cup (160 ml) whipping cream

Bittersweet chocolate ganache
7 oz. (200 g) bittersweet chocolate, 70 percent cocoa
1 ¼ cups (300 ml) whipping cream
2 ½ tablespoons (1 ¾ oz./50 g) honey

Decoration
1 sheet edible gold leaf

EQUIPMENT
1 whisk or handheld electric beater
1 cake mold, 8 in. (20 cm) diameter
1 long serrated knife
1 kitchen thermometer
1 flexible spatula
1 immersion blender
1 pastry ring, 8 ½ in. (22 cm) diameter
1 baking sheet lined with parchment paper
1 cake rack

A day ahead, prepare the ultra-shiny glaze.
Soften the sheets of gelatin in a bowl of cold water.

In a saucepan, combine the water, sugar, cocoa powder, and cream. Boil for about 1 minute.

Wring the water out of the gelatin and stir into the mixture. Chill overnight.

Prepare the chocolate cake layer.
Preheat the oven to 325°F (160°C). Butter the cake mold and dust it lightly with flour.

Make the chocolate cake batter following the method on p. 22, but using the ingredients listed above. Pour the batter into the prepared mold and bake for about 40 minutes, testing for doneness with the tip of a knife. The cake is cooked when it comes out dry.

Turn the cake out of the mold, leave to cool completely (otherwise it will be harder to cut), and cut it into three layers, using a long serrated knife, such as a bread knife.

Prepare the bittersweet chocolate ganache.
Follow the method on p. 21, using the ingredients listed above and omitting the butter.

Assemble the dessert.
Place the pastry ring on a flat, lined baking sheet. Position the first layer of chocolate cake; its diameter will be smaller than that of the pastry ring. Spread over one third of the ganache, then place another layer of chocolate cake over it, pressing down so that the ganache oozes out over the sides of the first cake layer. Spread the second third of the ganache, and repeat the procedure, finishing with a layer of ganache.

Rap lightly to smooth out the surface and freeze, ideally overnight.

The following day, decorate the dessert.
Reheat the ultra-shiny glaze over a bain-marie or gently in the microwave oven (on "defrost" or 500 W, stirring from time to time). Process with an

immersion blender. Take the frozen dessert out of the freezer and place it on a cake rack over a sheet of parchment paper that will catch the glaze that runs off. Cover the dessert completely with glaze and very lightly shake the cake rack to eliminate any excess glaze. Transfer the dessert to a serving dish and place the gold leaf in the center. Keep in the refrigerator for about 6 hours to defrost, and take it out an hour before serving so it comes to room temperature, when its flavors will be at their best.

Chocolate-Coated Cherries

MAKES 50 · PREPARATION TIME: 2 HOURS
RESTING AND SETTING TIME: 24 HOURS · MATURING TIME: 2 WEEKS

INGREDIENTS
50 cherries in *eau-de-vie* with their stalks
½ vanilla bean
10 ½ oz. (300 g) pastry fondant
10 ½ oz. (300 g) bittersweet chocolate,
  60 or 70 percent cocoa
Colored sugar

EQUIPMENT
1 cake rack or other rack
1 dish, larger than the cake rack
1 kitchen thermometer
1 baking sheet

Position a rack over a dish large enough to catch the *eau-de-vie* from the cherries. Drain the cherries on the rack for 1 to 2 hours, and finish drying them off on some sheets of paper towel.

Slit the half vanilla bean lengthwise and scrape out the seeds. In a heatproof bowl, combine the fondant, vanilla seeds, and 2 tablespoons of *eau-de-vie*. Heat over a bain-marie to 140°F–149°F (60°C–65°C), stirring constantly. Hold the cherries by their stalks and dip them in the fondant mixture, taking care to leave a little ring without any fondant. Place them on a baking sheet.

When the fondant has set, temper the chocolate (see pp. 13–15). Dip the cherries, including as much of the stalk as possible, one by one, in the chocolate (see p. 18).

Spead the colored sugar out on a baking sheet. Place the chocolate-coated cherries in the colored sugar and leave to set for at least 12 hours.

Chef's note
For optimal taste, prepare the cherries about 2 weeks before you intend serving them. The fondant will have melted, imbuing the cherries with heightened flavor.

Chocolate Profiteroles

SERVES 6–8 · PREPARATION TIME: 1 HOUR 20 MINUTES · COOKING TIME: 20 MINUTES

INGREDIENTS
Choux pastry
Scant ⅓ cup (75 ml) water
Scant ⅓ cup (75 ml) milk
Heaped ½ teaspoon (3 g) salt
¾ teaspoon (3 g) granulated sugar
4 tablespoons (2 oz./60 g) butter
1 cup (3 oz./90 g) cake flour
3 eggs, plus 1 egg yolk for glazing
A handful of sliced almonds for garnish

Chocolate sauce
1 ½ oz. (40 g) bittersweet chocolate, 60 percent cocoa
⅓ oz. (10 g) milk chocolate, 40 percent cocoa
⅓ cup (80 ml) whole milk
⅓ cup (80 ml) whipping cream

Vanilla-scented Chantilly cream
1 vanilla bean
⅔ cup (170 ml) whipping cream, well chilled
1 heaped tablespoon (15 g) sugar

To serve
2 pints (1 liter) ice cream (your choice of flavor)
Chocolate disks (optional)

EQUIPMENT
1 sieve
1 piping bag
1 baking sheet lined with parchment paper
1 pastry brush
1 flexible spatula
1 immersion blender
1 whisk or handheld electric beater
1 serrated knife

Prepare the choux pastry.
Preheat the oven to 480°F (250°C).

In a saucepan, bring the water, milk, salt, sugar, and butter to a boil. Sift the flour into the liquid. The important step is to dry it out: stir energetically until the moisture has evaporated. Remove from the heat and mix in the eggs, one by one. Stir thoroughly each time. When the consistency is right, it will have a satin sheen, like paint.

Spoon the batter into a piping bag and pipe out little rounds, just over ⅓ oz. (12 g) or 1 in. (2.5 cm) in diameter per choux on a lined baking sheet. For a nice finished result, brush the top of the dough with a beaten egg yolk and press down lightly with a fork. Scatter over a few sliced almonds.

Place the baking sheet in the oven and immediately switch off the heat.

As soon as the choux pastry begins to swell and color, turn the heat back to 350°F (180°C) and leave the pastries to dry out slowly for about 10 minutes.

Prepare the chocolate sauce.
Chop the two sorts of chocolate and melt them slowly in a bain-marie or in the microwave oven (on "defrost" or at 500 W maximum, stirring from time to time). Bring the milk and cream to a boil. Gradually pour a third of the boiling liquid over the melted chocolate. Using a flexible spatula, mix in energetically, drawing small circles to create an elastic, shiny "kernel." Incorporate the second third of the liquid, using the same procedure. Repeat with the last third. Process briefly using an immersion blender. Chill until ready to serve.

Prepare the vanilla-scented Chantilly cream.
Slit the vanilla bean lengthwise and scrape out the seeds into the well-chilled cream. Whip the cream with the sugar and vanilla seeds until it reaches the consistency of Chantilly cream.

Assemble the profiteroles.
Begin heating the chocolate sauce. Cut the tops off the choux pastries using a serrated knife. Place three pastries onto each plate. Fill one with the vanilla Chantilly cream and the two others with ice cream. Lightly sprinkle the tops with sugar and replace them over the fillings. Alternatively, cover with chocolate disks. Serve with hot chocolate sauce.

Melt-in-the-Mouth

Chocolate Tartlets

SERVES 6 · PREPARATION TIME: 40 MINUTES · COOKING TIME: 20 MINUTES

INGREDIENTS

Small quantity almond shortcrust pastry (see p. 186) or
  1 package sweet pie crust

Dulcey chocolate ganache

7 oz. (200 g) Valrhona Dulcey chocolate, 32 percent cocoa
Scant ½ cup (100 ml) heavy cream
2 teaspoons (15 g) honey

Decoration

3 ½ oz. (100 g) Valrhona Dulcey chocolate
⅜ teaspoon plus ¹⁄₁₆ teaspoon (¹⁄₂₈ oz./1 g) powdered
  cocoa butter

EQUIPMENT

1 rolling pin
4 sheets food-safe acetate
6 tartlet molds
1 flexible spatula
1 kitchen thermometer
1 baking sheet

Preheat the oven to 325°F (160°C). Prepare the almond shortcrust pastry, if using.

Line six tartlet molds with the store-bought pie crust or almond shortcrust pastry and bake in the oven for about 20 minutes until lightly golden.

Prepare the chocolate ganache.

Chop the Dulcey chocolate and melt it slowly in a bain-marie or in a microwave oven (on "defrost" or at 500 W maximum, stirring from time to time).

Bring the cream and honey to a boil in a saucepan. Slowly pour one third of the boiling mixture over the melted chocolate. Using a flexible spatula, briskly mix it in with a small circular movement to create an elastic, shiny "kernel." Then incorporate another third of the honey–cream mixture, using the same circular movement, and finally, the last third, still mixing with a circular movement.

Pour the ganache at 82°F–84°F (28°C–29°C) into the tartlet molds and let crystallize (harden) at 63°F (17°C).

Prepare the decoration.

Temper the Dulcey chocolate by adding cocoa butter (see p. 14). Using a little oil, stick a sheet of acetate to a flat baking sheet. Pour a small amount of chocolate onto the sheet, then immediately cover it with a second sheet of acetate. Using a rolling pin, roll out the couverture, spreading it toward the edges and making sure it is of equal thickness throughout. Before it has hardened, use a kitchen knife to cut out rectangles of different sizes and mold them around the rolling pin.

Let crystallize (harden) at 63°F (17°C).

Lay a curved rectangle of chocolate in the center of each tartlet.

Hazelnut Waves

SERVES 6–8 · PREPARATION TIME: 1 HOUR 30 MINUTES
COOKING TIME: 40 MINUTES · SETTING TIME: 3 HOURS · CHILLING TIME: 3 HOURS

INGREDIENTS

Milk chocolate ganache
8 oz. (225 g) milk chocolate, 40 percent cocoa
Scant ⅔ cup (150 ml) whipping cream
1 heaped tablespoon (1 oz./25 g) honey

Large quantity almond shortcrust pastry (see p. 186) or
   2 packages sweet pie crust

Hazelnut cream
7 tablespoons (3 ½ oz./100 g) butter
¾ cup (3 ½ oz./100 g) confectioners' sugar
1 tablespoon (⅓ oz./10 g) cornstarch

1 cup plus 3 tablespoons (3 ½ oz./100 g) finely ground
   hazelnuts
1 egg

EQUIPMENT
1 flexible spatula
1 rolling pin
2 sheets food-safe acetate
1 baking sheet, about 12 × 16 in. (30 × 40 cm)
1 piping bag fitted with a V-shaped tip, known as
   a Saint-Honoré tip

Prepare the milk chocolate ganache.

Chop the chocolate and melt it slowly in a bain-marie or in the microwave oven (on "defrost" or at 500 W maximum, stirring from time to time).

Bring the cream and honey to a boil in a saucepan. Gradually pour one third of the boiling cream over the melted chocolate. Using a flexible spatula, energetically mix the cream into the chocolate, drawing small, quick circles in the center to create a shiny, elastic "kernel."

Incorporate the second third of the cream and mix in exactly the same way. Pour in the remaining third, using the same stirring technique. Leave to set for 3 hours in a cool place, but do not chill in the refrigerator.

Prepare the almond shortcrust pastry (see p. 186), if using.

Alternatively, use store-bought sweet pie crust. Preheat the oven to 300°F–325°F (150°C–160°C). Roll the dough out to a thickness of ¼ in. (5 mm) to make a square or rectangular shape and bake on a baking sheet for about 20 minutes, until golden. Leave to cool.

Prepare the hazelnut cream.

Soften the butter in a mixing bowl. Sift the confectioners' sugar and cornstarch together and add to the butter, stirring constantly. Stir as you add the ground hazelnuts, then the egg.

Preheat the oven to 375°F (190°C).

Spread the hazelnut cream over the entire surface of the cooled almond pastry and bake for about 20 minutes, until a nice golden color. Leave to cool completely.

Spoon the chocolate ganache into a piping bag fitted with a V-shaped or angled tip, and pipe over the hazelnut cream to form a wave pattern. Leave to set in the refrigerator for about 3 hours.

Remove from the refrigerator, and using a heated knife (dip it in hot water and then dry it carefully), cut out rectangles measuring 1 ¼ × 3 in. (3 × 8 cm).

Chef's note

As soon as you remove the pastry from the oven, place a sheet of parchment paper over the top, and then place a baking sheet on top. This will ensure that the surface remains perfectly smooth as it cools.

Tonka Bean–Scented Ivory Panna Cotta with Strawberry Coulis

SERVES 8 · PREPARATION TIME: 40 MINUTES · CHILLING TIME: OVERNIGHT

INGREDIENTS

Ivory panna cotta
2 sheets (4 g) gelatin
6 oz. (175 g) white chocolate, 35 percent cocoa
¾ cup (200 ml) milk
1 ¼ cups (300 ml) whipping cream
½ tonka bean

Strawberry coulis
4 ⅔ oz. (130 g) strawberries
1 cup (250 ml) water
2 tablespoons (1 oz./25 g) granulated sugar

EQUIPMENT
1 flexible spatula
1 grater
1 immersion blender
8 silicone molds or small glasses
1 colander

A day ahead, prepare the white chocolate panna cotta.

Soften the gelatin in a bowl of cold water. Chop the chocolate and melt it gently in a bain-marie or in the microwave oven (on "defrost" or at 500 W maximum, stirring from time to time).

Bring the milk to a boil. Wring the excess water out of the gelatin and dissolve it in the hot milk. Remove from the heat immediately.

Slowly pour one third of the hot mixture over the melted chocolate. Using a flexible spatula, briskly mix it in with a small circular movement to create an elastic, shiny "kernel." Then incorporate another third of the hot liquid, using the same circular movement, and finally, the last third, still mixing with a circular movement. Pour in the cold whipping cream and grate the half tonka bean into the mixture. Process with an immersion blender until the mixture is perfectly smooth and emulsified.

Wait until it just starts to thicken before you pour it into silicone molds or small glasses. This will ensure that the grated tonka bean does not rise directly to the surface. Chill overnight.

Prepare the strawberry coulis.

Set aside several whole strawberries for garnish and cut the others into small pieces. Leave them in a mixing bowl. Bring the water and sugar to a boil and pour the syrup over the cut strawberries. Chill overnight.

The next day, carefully pour the strawberries into a colander over a bowl to catch the juice. It should be perfectly transparent, so make sure you don't crush any strawberries into it. Drizzle the juice over the panna cotta and garnish with a few strawberry halves. Serve cold.

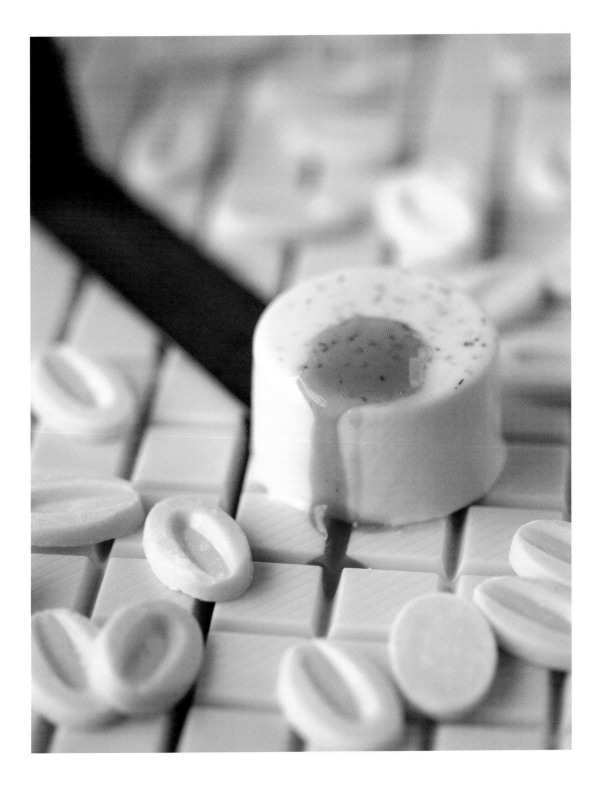

Soy Milk Nama Choco

SERVES 6–8 · PREPARATION TIME: 15 MINUTES · CHILLING TIME: 3 HOURS

INGREDIENTS

12 oz. (350 g) bittersweet chocolate, 70 percent cocoa
1 cup (250 ml) soy milk
1 ½ teaspoons (10 g) honey
1 ½ teaspoons (10 g) glucose syrup
1 cup minus 1 ½ tablespoons (6 ⅓ oz./180 g) light brown (*cassonade*) or colored sugar

EQUIPMENT

1 flexible spatula
1 immersion blender
1 confectionery frame or brownie pan, lined with plastic wrap
1 baking sheet lined with parchment paper

Chop the chocolate and melt it slowly in a bain-marie or in the microwave oven (on "defrost" or at 500 W maximum, stirring from time to time).

Bring the soy milk to a boil with the honey and glucose syrup. Gradually pour a third of the boiling mixture over the melted chocolate. Using a flexible spatula, mix in energetically, drawing small circles to create an elastic, shiny "kernel." Incorporate the second third of the liquid, using the same procedure. Repeat with the last third. Process for a few seconds using an immersion blender so that the mixture is smooth and perfectly emulsified.

Pour the mixture into the frame positioned on the lined baking sheet, or into the prepared brownie pan. Chill for a minimum of 3 hours.

Remove the frame, sprinkle the ganache with the light brown or colored sugar, and cut out cubes of 1 in. (2 cm).

Chef's note

This is a version of a ganache that is popular in Japan. Prepared in this way, it can be used as a bonbon.

Bittersweet Chocolate Panna Cotta with Thai-Style Lemongrass Foam

**SERVES 6–8 · PREPARATION TIME: 1 HOUR 45 MINUTES
COOKING TIME: 10 MINUTES · CHILLING TIME: OVERNIGHT PLUS 4 HOURS**

INGREDIENTS

Bittersweet chocolate panna cotta
2 sheets (4 g) gelatin
4 ⅔ oz. (130 g) bittersweet chocolate, 60 percent cocoa
¾ cup (200 ml) milk
1 ¼ cups (300 ml) whipping cream

Pineapple sticks
14 oz. (400 g) fresh pineapple
1 tablespoon plus 2 teaspoons (20 g) light brown sugar (*cassonade*)
⅔ cup (150 ml) pineapple juice
1 tablespoon (15 ml) brown rum

Thai-style lemongrass foam
2 cups (500 ml) whole milk

¼ cup (1 ¾ oz./50 g) granulated sugar
3 sticks lemongrass
½ vanilla bean
2 sheets (4 g) gelatin
½ cup (120 ml) unsweetened coconut milk

EQUIPMENT
1 flexible spatula
1 immersion blender
8 shot glasses, preferably square
1 ovenproof dish
1 chinois (fine sieve)
1 siphon

A day ahead, prepare the bittersweet chocolate panna cotta.
Soften the gelatin in a bowl of very cold water. Chop the chocolate and melt it slowly in a bain-marie or in the microwave oven (on "defrost" or at 500 W maximum, stirring from time to time).

Bring the milk and cream to a boil. When the gelatin has softened, wring out the water and dissolve it in the milk–cream mixture. Remove from the heat as soon as it has dissolved. Slowly pour one third of the hot mixture over the melted chocolate. Using a flexible spatula, briskly mix it in with a small circular movement to create an elastic, shiny "kernel." Then incorporate another third of the hot liquid, using the same circular movement, and finally, the last third, still mixing with a circular movement. Process with an immersion blender to ensure that the mixture is smooth and well emulsified. Pour into shot glasses and chill overnight.

The next day, prepare the pineapple sticks.
Preheat the oven to 425°F (210°C–220°C).

Peel and core the pineapple and cut it into little sticks. Combine the pineapple sticks with the light brown sugar, pineapple juice, and rum, and place in an ovenproof dish. Bake in the oven for about 10 minutes.

Prepare the Thai-style lemongrass foam.
Bring the milk and sugar to a boil and reduce until 1 ½ cups (350 ml) remain.

Thinly slice the lemongrass sticks, setting some aside for garnish. Slit the half vanilla bean lengthwise and scrape out the seeds. Incorporate these two flavorings into the reduced milk. Leave to infuse for 30 minutes and strain through a chinois (fine sieve). Soften the gelatin in a bowl of cold water. Wring out the excess water and dissolve it in the warm flavored milk. Stir in the

coconut milk and pour the liquid into a siphon. Set aside in the refrigerator to chill for at least 3 to 4 hours.

To serve, arrange the pineapple sticks over the panna cotta in the glasses, then press out the foam from the siphon to fill the glasses. Garnish with thin slices of lemongrass.

Verrines of Hot Chocolate Mousse, Crème Brûlée, and Berry Preserve

SERVES 6–8 · PREPARATION TIME: 45 MINUTES · COOKING TIME: 20 MINUTES · CHILLING TIME: 35 MINUTES

INGREDIENTS
Vanilla crème brûlée
¼ cup (65 ml) whole milk
¼ cup (1 ¾ oz./50 g) granulated sugar
1 vanilla bean
⅔ cup plus 2 teaspoons (190 ml) whipping cream,
  well chilled
4 egg yolks

Hot bittersweet chocolate mousse
2 ¾ oz. (80 g) bittersweet chocolate, 70 percent cocoa
2 tablespoons (1 oz./25 g) granulated sugar

½ teaspoon (1 g) agar-agar powder
½ cup plus 2 teaspoons (135 ml) whole milk

Berry preserve

EQUIPMENT
1 sieve
8 ovenproof shot glasses or small bowls
1 flexible spatula
1 siphon
1 kitchen thermometer

Prepare the vanilla crème brûlée.
Preheat the oven to 200°F (95°C). Bring the milk and sugar to a boil in a saucepan. Slit the vanilla bean and scrape the seeds out into the hot milk. Leave to infuse for a few minutes and then strain through a sieve.

Combine the chilled cream with the egg yolks. Pour the vanilla-infused milk over this mixture and mix thoroughly. Pour it into the glasses and bake for about 17–20 minutes, until the surface offers some resistance to the touch but the interior is not liquid. Chill for 30 minutes.

Prepare the hot bittersweet chocolate mousse.
Chop the chocolate and melt it slowly in a bain-marie or in the microwave oven (on "defrost" or at 500 W maximum, stirring from time to time).

Combine the sugar and agar-agar, then stir into the milk and bring to a boil.

Gradually pour one third of the boiling liquid over the melted chocolate. Using a flexible spatula, mix it in energetically, drawing small circles to create an elastic, shiny "kernel." Incorporate the second third of the liquid, using the same procedure. Repeat with the last third. Pour the hot mixture into a siphon, keeping it in a bain-marie at 113°F–122°F (45°C–50°C) so that you can serve it hot.

Place a spoonful of berry preserve on the top of the vanilla crèmes brûlées and return to the refrigerator. Just before serving, press out the hot chocolate mousse from the siphon to cover the preserve.

Chef's notes
It's essential to allow the agar-agar to boil, otherwise it will have no jelling strength.

Grate a few chocolate shavings over the mousse for a nice textural contrast—you'll have both melting softness and crunch.

Jelled Milk Chocolate, Chestnuts, and Soy Foam

SERVES 6–8 · PREPARATION TIME: 45 MINUTES · COOKING TIME: 10 MINUTES · CHILLING TIME: OVERNIGHT

INGREDIENTS

Soy-milk foam
2 sheets (4 g) gelatin
⅓ cup (75 ml) milk
3 ½ tablespoons (1 ½ oz./40 g) sugar
⅔ cup (180 ml) soy milk
2 tablespoons (30 ml) whipping cream

Jelled milk chocolate
1 sheet (2 g) gelatin
2 ⅔ oz. (75 g) milk chocolate, 40 percent cocoa
⅔ cup (175 ml) milk
2 ½ teaspoons (10 g) sugar

Small quantity almond streusel (see p. 187) or 1 packet
 shortbread cookies, roughly crushed

Chestnut vermicelli
4 ¼ oz. (120 g) creamed chestnut (*crème de marron*,
 available at specialty stores or online)
5 ½ tablespoons (2 ¾ oz./80 g) butter, softened
Rum, according to taste (optional)

6–8 disks of milk chocolate, 40 percent cocoa

EQUIPMENT
1 siphon
1 flexible spatula
1 immersion blender
6–8 shot glasses (*verrines*)
1 baking sheet
1 piping bag fitted with a plain ⅛ in. (3 mm) tip

A day ahead, prepare the soy-milk foam.
Soften the gelatin in a bowl filled with cold water. Combine the milk, sugar, soy milk, and cream in a saucepan and bring to a boil. Remove from the heat, wring the water out of the gelatin, and incorporate it into the hot liquid. Leave to cool and pour the mixture into the siphon. Chill overnight.

Prepare the jelled milk chocolate.
Soften the gelatin in a bowl filled with cold water.

 Chop the chocolate and melt it slowly in a bain-marie or in the microwave oven (on "defrost" or at 500 W maximum, stirring from time to time).

 Bring the milk and sugar to a boil in a saucepan. Remove from the heat, wring the water out of the gelatin, and incorporate it into the hot mixture.

 Gradually pour one third of the hot milk over the melted chocolate. Using a flexible spatula, mix in energetically, drawing small circles to create an elastic, shiny "kernel." Incorporate the second third of the liquid, using the same procedure. Repeat with the last third. Process for a few seconds using an immersion blender so that the mixture is smooth and perfectly emulsified.

 Pour the chocolate mixture into the glasses and set aside in the refrigerator.

Prepare the almond streusel (see p. 187), if using.

Just before serving, prepare the chestnut vermicelli mixture.
Combine the chestnut cream with the softened butter and add a little rum, if using. Spoon it into a piping bag fitted with a plain ⅛ in. (3 mm) tip.

To serve, place 1 chocolate disk at a slight angle in the glass of jelled milk chocolate. Sprinkle with streusel or roughly crushed cookies and pipe over the chestnut mixture. Top with soy foam.

Warm Chocolate Tart

SERVES 6 · PREPARATION TIME: 1 HOUR · COOKING TIME: 25 MINUTES
CHILLING TIME: 2 HOURS 30 MINUTES

INGREDIENTS
Small quantity almond shortcrust pastry (see p. 186) or
  1 package sweet pie crust

Baked bittersweet ganache
4 ¼ oz. (120 g) bittersweet chocolate, 70 percent cocoa
½ cup plus 2 tablespoons (150 ml) milk
½ cup plus 2 tablespoons (150 ml) whipping cream
3 ½ tablespoons (1 ½ oz./40 g) sugar
2 egg yolks

A little unsweetened cocoa powder for dusting

EQUIPMENT
1 rolling pin
2 sheets food-safe acetate
1 tart mold or pan, 7 in. (18 cm) diameter
1 flexible spatula
1 piping bag

Prepare the almond shortcrust pastry (see p. 186), if using.

Alternatively, use a store-bought sweet pie crust. Preheat the oven to 300°F–325°F (150°C–160°C). Line a tart pan with the pastry, refrigerate for 30 minutes, then bake for about 20 minutes until the pastry turns a golden color.

Prepare the bittersweet chocolate ganache.

Chop the chocolate and melt it slowly in a bain-marie or in the microwave oven (on "defrost" or at 500 W maximum, stirring from time to time).

Bring the milk, cream, and sugar to a boil in a saucepan. Gradually pour one third of the boiling liquid over the melted chocolate. Using a flexible spatula, energetically mix the liquid into the chocolate, drawing small, quick circles in the center to create a shiny, elastic "kernel." Incorporate the second third of the liquid and mix in exactly the same way. Pour in the remaining third, using the same stirring technique. Incorporate the egg yolks and chill for at least 1 hour.

Preheat the oven to 350°F–375°F (180°C–190°C). Spoon the ganache into a piping bag and pipe it out into the tart shell. Bake for 5 to 7 minutes.

Dust lightly with cocoa powder and serve immediately.

Mandarin Marvels

MAKES 20–30 MINI TARTLETS · PREPARATION TIME: 2 HOURS
COOKING TIME: 15 MINUTES · RESTING TIME: 40 MINUTES · CHILLING TIME: 2 HOURS

INGREDIENTS

1 quantity spiced dough (see p. 187) or 1 package sweet pie crust

Bittersweet chocolate ganache

3 ½ oz. (100 g) bittersweet chocolate, 60 percent cocoa
½ cup plus 1 ½ tablespoons (150 ml) whipping cream
1 heaped tablespoon (1 oz./25 g) honey

Decoration

10 seedless mandarins
1 bar bittersweet chocolate, 60 percent cocoa

EQUIPMENT

1 flexible spatula
1 whisk or handheld electric beater (optional)
Plastic wrap
Rolling pin
2 sheets food-safe acetate
20–30 mini tartlet molds
1 immersion blender
1 well-sharpened paring knife
1 vegetable peeler

Prepare the spiced dough (see p. 187), if using.

Alternatively, use store-bought sweet pie crust. Preheat the oven to 350°F (170°C). Cut the spiced dough or pie crust to fit the mini tartlet molds. Bake the tartlet cases for about 15 minutes. Let cool.

Prepare the bittersweet chocolate ganache.

Chop the chocolate and melt it slowly in a bain-marie or in the microwave oven (on "defrost" or at 500 W maximum, stirring from time to time).

Bring the cream and honey to a boil in a saucepan. Gradually pour one third of the boiling cream over the melted chocolate. Using a flexible spatula, energetically mix the cream into the chocolate, drawing small, quick circles in the center to create a shiny, elastic "kernel." Incorporate the second third of the cream and mix in exactly the same way. Pour in the remaining third, using the same stirring technique. Process with an immersion blender until the mixture is smooth and perfectly emulsified. Pour the ganache into the cooled tartlet shells.

Prepare the mandarin segments.

Using a well-sharpened paring knife, peel the mandarins, making sure you remove all the white pith. Extract the segments. Hold the mandarin in the hollow of your hand and slip the knife along the membrane that encloses the segment until you reach the center of the fruit. Repeat on the other side of the segment, all along the membrane to the center. The segment will come out on its own. Repeat with the remaining segments and reserve them on some sheets of paper towel.

To serve, arrange four or five segments on each tartlet to reproduce the shape of a half-mandarin. Decorate with a few chocolate shavings: scrape them off from the bar of chocolate using the tip of a vegetable peeler. Keep in the refrigerator until ready to serve.

Sunny Pear and Chocolate Tart

SERVES 8 · PREPARATION TIME: 45 MINUTES · COOKING TIME: 30 MINUTES
CHILLING TIME: 1 HOUR 30 MINUTES

INGREDIENTS

Large quantity almond shortcrust pastry (see p. 186) or
  1 package sweet pie crust

Honey-softened pears

4 finely flavored pears, such as Bartlett (Williams' Bon
  Chrétien) or Doyenne du Comice
Scant ⅓ cup (3 ½ oz./100 g) honey

Chocolate filling

1 ½ oz. (40 g) bittersweet chocolate, 70 percent cocoa
¼ cup plus 1 teaspoon (65 ml) whole milk
½ cup (125 ml) whipping cream

½ vanilla bean
1 egg
2 tablespoons (1 oz./25 g) granulated sugar

EQUIPMENT

1 rolling pin
2 sheets food-safe acetate
1 tart mold or pan, 8 in. (20 cm) diameter
Cookie cutters or small glasses, various sizes
1 baking sheet
1 whisk
1 immersion blender

Prepare the almond shortcrust pastry (see p. 186), if using.

Alternatively, use store-bought sweet pie crust. Preheat the oven to 300°F–325°F (150°C–160°C). Butter the tart mold. Roll the dough out to a thickness of ⅛ in. (3 mm) and line the tart pan. Roll out the remaining pieces of dough to just under ¹⁄₁₆ in. (2 mm) and using differently sized cookie cutters, cut out small disks to use for decoration. Place the disks on a baking sheet. Chill all the dough for 30 minutes.

Bake the tart case and disks until the pastry turns a golden color—about 15 to 20 minutes for the tart case. The disks will bake quickly—keep an eye on them so you can remove them when they are the right color, and leave them to cool.

Prepare the honey-softened pears.

Peel the pears, cut them into halves, then cut these into four or five pieces, depending on their size. Using a kitchen knife, remove the core and seeds, making sure the cut pieces are all the same size. Heat the honey slightly in a saucepan until it just begins to caramelize. Add the pear pieces and turn them over in the honey to coat them. Leave to cook gently for 2 to 3 minutes then drain and set aside.

Prepare the chocolate filling.

Chop the chocolate. Pour the milk and cream into a saucepan. Slit the half vanilla bean and scrape the seeds out into the liquid. Bring the mixture to a boil, remove from the heat, and let cool until it is lukewarm. Whisk in the egg, then the sugar and chopped chocolate. Process with an immersion blender until thoroughly combined and set aside.

When the tart shell is golden, ensure that the oven temperature is lowered to 300°F (150°C) if you have used the higher temperature. Arrange the pear slices attractively around the shell. Pour the chocolate filling in, pouring into the center, and continue baking for 10 to 12 minutes.

As soon as the filling has set, remove the tart from the oven and leave to cool at room temperature. When cool, place in the refrigerator for at least 1 hour. Bring to room temperature before serving.

Royal

SERVES 6–8 · PREPARATION TIME: 2 HOURS · COOKING TIME: 10–12 MINUTES
CHILLING TIME: 6 HOURS · FREEZING TIME: 13 HOURS

INGREDIENTS

Almond *dacquoise*
Generous ⅓ cup (1 ¼ oz./35 g) cake flour
1 cup plus 3 tablespoons (3 ½ oz./100 g) ground almonds
Scant cup (4 ¼ oz./120 g) confectioners' sugar
6 (6 oz./170 g) egg whites
⅓ cup (2 oz./60 g) granulated sugar

Crisp praline
⅔ oz. (20 g) milk chocolate, 40 percent cocoa
3 ½ oz. (100 g) praline
1 ½ oz. (40 g) crushed *crêpes dentelles* (an extremely friable, fine wafer-like cookie: a Breton specialty)

Custard-based bittersweet chocolate mousse
3 ¾ oz. (110 g) bittersweet chocolate, 70 percent cocoa

1 egg yolk
2 ½ teaspoons (⅓ oz./10 g) sugar
Scant ¼ cup (50 ml) whole milk
Scant 1 ½ cups (350 ml) whipping cream, divided as follows:
  ⅔ cup (150 ml) plus ¾ cup (200 ml)

EQUIPMENT
1 sieve
1 whisk or handheld electric beater
1 flexible spatula
1 jelly (Swiss) roll baking pan lined with parchment paper or silicone baking mat
1 pastry ring, 6 ½ in. (16 cm) diameter
1 kitchen thermometer
1 immersion blender

Prepare the almond *dacquoise*.
Preheat the oven to 350°F–375°F (180°C–190°C). Sift the flour with the ground almonds and the confectioners' sugar into a mixing bowl. Begin whisking the egg whites with the granulated sugar, until soft peaks form. Carefully fold in the sifted dry ingredients with a flexible spatula. Spread it out evenly over the lined baking pan or silicone mat. Bake for about 10 minutes, until a nice golden color.

Prepare the crisp praline.
Chop the chocolate and melt it slowly in a bain-marie or in the microwave oven (on "defrost" or at 500 W maximum, stirring from time to time). Incorporate the praline into the melted chocolate and then carefully stir in the crushed *crêpes dentelles*.

Cut the *dacquoise* base out into a circle just slightly smaller than the pastry ring and cover it with the crisp praline. Place in the refrigerator.

Prepare the custard-based chocolate mousse.
Chop the chocolate up and melt it slowly in a bain-marie or in the microwave oven (on "defrost" or at 500 W maximum, stirring from time to time).

In a mixing bowl, beat the egg yolk with the sugar until thick and pale. Pour this mixture into a saucepan, add the milk and ⅔ cup (150 ml) whipping cream, and simmer over low heat. The liquid should thicken slightly and coat the back of a spoon. The temperature should be 180°F–183°F (82°C–84°C). Remove from the heat and pour the custard into a deep mixing bowl. Process for a few seconds with an immersion blender for a smooth, creamy texture. Gradually pour one third of the hot custard over the melted chocolate. Using a flexible spatula, mix it in energetically, drawing small circles to create an elastic, shiny "kernel." Incorporate the second third of the custard, using the same procedure. Repeat with the last third. Process with an immersion blender for a smooth, creamy texture.

Using a whisk or an electric beater, whip ¾ cup (200 ml) well-chilled cream until it is just lightly whipped. When the chocolate custard reaches a temperature of 113°F–122°F (45°C–50°C), fold in one third of the softly whipped cream. Carefully fold in the remaining cream with a flexible spatula.

Assemble the royal.

Position the *dacquoise* and crisp praline layer in the center of the ring. Pour in the chocolate mousse, ensuring that you reserve a little for the decoration. Place in the freezer immediately. As soon as the mousse begins to set, prepare decorations with the remaining mousse and arrange over the top. Freeze for about 12 hours.

Remove the pastry ring. Place in the refrigerator for at least 6 hours. Serve it only when it is completely defrosted.

Crunchy

Extraordinarily Chocolaty Tart

SERVES 6–8 · PREPARATION TIME: 1 HOUR · COOKING TIME: 20 MINUTES
CHILLING TIME: 2 HOURS 30 MINUTES

INGREDIENTS

Small quantity almond shortcrust pastry (see p. 186) or
  1 package sweet pie crust

Bittersweet chocolate ganache
12 ⅓ oz. (350 g) bittersweet chocolate, 70 percent cocoa
1 cup (250 ml) whipping cream
1 tablespoon (15 ml) acacia honey
3 tablespoons plus 1 teaspoon (1 ¾ oz./50 g) butter, diced

A little melted chocolate to brush the tart shell

EQUIPMENT
1 rolling pin
2 sheets food-safe acetate or parchment paper
1 tart pan, 8 in. (20 cm) diameter
1 flexible spatula
1 kitchen thermometer
1 immersion blender
1 pastry brush

Prepare the almond shortcrust pastry (see p. 186), if using.
Alternatively, use store-bought sweet pie crust. Preheat the oven to 300°F–325°F (150°C–160°C). Line a tart pan with the pastry, refrigerate for 30 minutes, then bake for about 20 minutes until golden.

Prepare the bittersweet chocolate ganache.
Chop the chocolate and melt it slowly in a bain-marie or in the microwave oven (on "defrost" or at 500 W maximum, stirring from time to time).

Bring the cream to a boil with the honey. Gradually pour one third of the boiling cream over the melted chocolate. Using a flexible spatula, mix in energetically, drawing small circles to create an elastic, shiny "kernel." Incorporate the second third of the cream–honey mixture, using the same procedure. Repeat with the last third.

When the temperature cools to 95°F–104°F (35°C–40°C), stir in the diced butter. Process for a few seconds using an immersion blender so that the mixture is smooth and perfectly emulsified.

Brush a fine layer of melted chocolate over the cooled tart shell to seal it. As soon as it has hardened, pour the ganache into the shell and chill for about 2 hours. Serve it at room temperature.

Be sure to eat this tart the day you make it if you want to enjoy the crisp pastry and creamy ganache at their best.

Golden Rules

SERVES 6–8 · PREPARATION TIME: 1 HOUR · COOKING TIME: 20 MINUTES
CHILLING TIME: 3 HOURS 30 MINUTES

INGREDIENTS
Large quantity almond shortcrust pastry (see p. 186) or
  1 package sweet pie crust
3 tablespoons orange or grapefruit preserve

Bittersweet chocolate ganache
Either 5 ½ oz. (150 g) bittersweet chocolate,
  70 percent cocoa
Or 5 ⅔ oz. (160 g) bittersweet chocolate, 60 percent cocoa
Generous ½ cup (150 ml) whipping cream
3 tablespoons plus 1 teaspoon (1 ¾ oz./50 g) salted butter,
  diced, plus some melted butter to fix the rulers onto the
  baking sheet

Decoration
Edible gold leaf

EQUIPMENT
1 rolling pin
2 sheets of food-safe acetate or parchment paper
2 confectionery or four-sided rulers, ½ in. (1 cm) high
1 baking sheet lined with parchment paper
Plastic wrap or aluminum foil
1 flexible spatula
1 kitchen thermometer
1 immersion blender
1 piping bag (optional)

Prepare the almond shortcrust pastry (see p. 186), if using.

Alternatively, use store-bought sweet pie crust. Preheat the oven to 300°F–325°F (150°C–160°C). Roll out the pastry and form two long rectangles. Position them between two confectionery rulers buttered in place on a baking sheet lined with parchment paper. Press the pastry against the rulers to form sides.

Chill for 30 minutes and bake for about 20 minutes until the pastry is a nice golden color. When it has cooled, drizzle a stripe of orange or grapefruit preserve down the center. Close each end of the hollow with plastic wrap or aluminum foil.

Prepare the bittersweet chocolate ganache.

Chop the chocolate and melt it slowly in a bain-marie or in the microwave oven (on "defrost" or at 500 W maximum, stirring from time to time).

Bring the cream to a boil in a saucepan. Gradually pour one third of the boiling cream over the melted chocolate. Using a flexible spatula, energetically mix the cream into the chocolate, drawing small, quick circles in the center to create a shiny, elastic "kernel." Incorporate the second third of the cream and mix in exactly the same way. Pour in the remaining third, using the same stirring technique.

As soon as the ganache cools to a temperature of 95°F–104°F (35°C–40°C), add the diced butter. Process with an immersion blender so that the mixture is smooth and perfectly emulsified.

Spoon or pipe out the ganache into the pastry hollow. Rap the baking sheet lightly to ensure that the ganache is level and leave in the refrigerator to set for 3 hours.

When the ganache has set, remove the aluminum foil or plastic wrap on either end and cut the "rules" to the desired size. Decorate with edible gold leaf.

Walnut, Caramel, and Coffee–Chocolate Tart

SERVES 8 · PREPARATION TIME: 45 MINUTES · COOKING TIME: 20 MINUTES
CHILLING TIME: 2 HOURS 30 MINUTES

INGREDIENTS

Large quantity almond shortcrust pastry (see p. 186) or
  1 package sweet pie crust

Walnut and caramel layer

2 ¼ oz. (60 g) milk chocolate, 40 percent cocoa
1 ¾ oz. (50 g) walnuts
½ cup minus 1 tablespoon (110 ml) whipping cream
⅓ cup (2 ½ oz./70 g) granulated sugar
2 tablespoons (1 oz./30 g) butter

Coffee ganache

2 ¾ oz. (80 g) bittersweet chocolate, 60 percent cocoa
Scant ⅓ cup (70 ml) whipping cream
1 ½ teaspoons (10 g) acacia honey
1 tablespoon (3 ½ g) instant coffee granules
1 tablespoon (15 g) butter

EQUIPMENT

1 rolling pin
2 sheets food-safe acetate or parchment paper
1 tart pan, 8 in. (20 cm) diameter
1 flexible spatula
1 kitchen thermometer
1 immersion blender

Prepare the almond shortcrust pastry (see p. 186), if using.

Alternatively, use store-bought sweet pie crust. Preheat the oven to 300°F–325°F (150°C–160°C). Line a tart pan with the pastry, refrigerate for 30 minutes, then bake for about 20 minutes until the pastry turns a golden color.

Prepare the walnut and caramel layer.

Chop the milk chocolate and roughly chop the nuts. Bring the cream to a boil. Place one third of the sugar in a heavy-bottomed saucepan. Cook until it forms a light caramel. Add the next third of the sugar and stir. When this quantity has reached the same color—a light caramel—add the last third of the sugar. When the caramel is ready, carefully add the butter and hot cream, taking care not to splash yourself as the caramel will be very hot. The cream is heated before adding so that the caramel doesn't harden. Leave to boil briefly. Incorporate the chopped chocolate and then stir in the chopped nuts. Pour the mixture into the cooled tart shell and set aside. It will set very quickly.

Prepare the coffee ganache.

Chop the chocolate and melt it slowly in a bain-marie or in the microwave oven (on "defrost" or at 500 W maximum, stirring from time to time).

Bring the cream, honey, and instant coffee to a boil. Gradually pour one third of the boiling mixture over the melted chocolate. Using a flexible spatula, mix it in energetically, drawing small circles to create an elastic, shiny "kernel." Incorporate the second third of the liquid, using the same procedure. Repeat with the last third.

Keep an eye on the temperature. As soon as the ganache cools to 95°F–104°F (35°C–40°C), add the butter, mixing in thoroughly. Process briefly with an immersion blender. Pour it directly over the walnut–caramel layer and leave to set for about 2 hours in the refrigerator.

A Take on Tartlets

SERVES 8 · PREPARATION TIME: 45 MINUTES
CHILLING TIME: OVERNIGHT · FREEZING TIME: 1 HOUR · COOKING TIME: 20 MINUTES

INGREDIENTS

Bittersweet chocolate *crémeux*

4 ¼ oz. (120 g) bittersweet chocolate, 70 percent cocoa
3 egg yolks
2 tablespoons (1 oz./25 g) granulated sugar
½ cup plus 1 teaspoon (130 ml) whole milk
½ cup plus 1 teaspoon (130 ml) whipping cream

Large quantity almond shortcrust pastry (see p. 186) or
1 packet (approx. 32 cookies) Breton *galettes* (shortbread cookies)

EQUIPMENT

1 whisk or handheld electric beater
1 kitchen thermometer
1 immersion blender
1 flexible spatula
Plastic wrap
2 sheets food-safe acetate or parchment paper
1 baking sheet
1 round cookie cutter or 1 glass, 2–2 ½ in. (5–6 cm) diameter
1 piping bag fitted with a large plain ½ in. (14–16 mm) tip

A day ahead, prepare the bittersweet chocolate *crémeux*.

Chop the chocolate and melt it slowly in a bain-marie or in the microwave oven (on "defrost" or at 500 W maximum, stirring from time to time).

While it is melting, prepare the custard (*crème anglaise*). Whisk the egg yolks and sugar together. Pour this mixture into a saucepan with the milk and cream and cook over low heat until it is slightly thickened and coats the back of a spoon. The temperature should be 180°F–183°F (82°C–84°C). Remove the saucepan from the heat and pour the custard into a deep bowl. Process for a few seconds with an immersion blender until the texture is smooth and creamy.

Slowly pour one third of the hot custard over the melted chocolate. Using a flexible spatula, energetically mix the custard into the chocolate, drawing small, quick circles in the center to create a shiny, elastic "kernel." Incorporate the second third of the custard and mix in exactly the same way. Pour in the remaining third, using the same stirring technique. Use an immersion blender to finish the emulsifying process.

Pour it into a bowl and cover with plastic wrap flush with the surface to prevent a skin from forming. Chill overnight.

The next day, prepare the almond shortcrust pastry (see p. 186), if using.

Roll the pastry dough out to a thickness of ⅛ in. (3 mm) between two sheets of acetate. Using a round, 2–2 ½ in. (5–6 cm) diameter cookie cutter or a glass, cut out 16 disks from the pastry dough. Place in the freezer for about 1 hour, ensuring that the disks are flat. When the dough has completely hardened, place the disks on a baking sheet.

Preheat the oven to 300°F–325°F (150°C–160°C) and bake for about 15 minutes, until the pastry is a nice golden color. Place on a cooling rack to cool.

When the disks are cool, fill a piping bag fitted with a large plain ½ in. (14–16 mm) tip with the chocolate *crémeux* and pipe a large ball onto a pastry circle, or a Breton cookie if using. Top with another circle or cookie and press down lightly so that the chocolate cream is flush with the edge. Repeat the procedure with the remaining disks of pastry or cookies.

Coffee, Chocolate, and Vanilla Creams with Shortbread

SERVES 6–8 · PREPARATION TIME: 1 HOUR
COOKING TIME: 15 MINUTES · CHILLING TIME: 3 HOURS 30 MINUTES

INGREDIENTS
Breton shortbread (see p. 188) or 1 packet shortbread cookies

Basic pouring custard (*crème anglaise*)
8 egg yolks
Scant ½ cup (2 ¾ oz./80 g) sugar
1 ½ cups (380 ml) whole milk
1 ½ cups (380 ml) whipping cream

Coffee cream
1 lb. (500 g) basic pouring custard, made using ingredients above
3 tablespoons (⅓ oz./10 g) instant coffee granules

Chocolate *crémeux*
1 lb. (500 g) basic pouring custard, made using ingredients above
7 oz. (200 g) bittersweet chocolate, 60 percent cocoa

Vanilla-scented Chantilly cream
¾ cup (200 ml) whipping cream, well chilled
½ vanilla bean
2 ½ tablespoons (⅔ oz./20 g) sugar

EQUIPMENT
1 handheld electric beater
1 rolling pin
2 sheets food-safe acetate or parchment paper
1 baking sheet
8 shot glasses or small bowls
1 whisk
1 kitchen thermometer
1 flexible spatula
1 immersion blender
1 chinois (fine sieve)

Prepare the Breton shortbread (see p. 188), if using.
If you are using store-bought shortbread cookies, crumble them roughly. Place a few cubes of homemade shortbread or a little of the crumbled cookies in the bottom of each glass or bowl.

Prepare the pouring custard.
Whisk the egg yolks and sugar together until pale and thick. Pour the mixture into a saucepan and add the milk and cream. Cook slowly over low heat, stirring constantly until the mixture has thickened slightly and coats the back of a spoon. The temperature should be between 180°F–187°F (82°C–86°C); remove the saucepan from the heat as soon as the thermometer shows 180°F (82°C), because the temperature will continue to rise. As soon as you have removed the custard from the heat, pour it into a deep bowl and process briefly with an immersion blender for a smooth, creamy texture.

Prepare the coffee cream.
Weigh out 1 lb. (500 g) of hot pouring custard. Stir in the instant coffee until it is completely dissolved. Set aside in the refrigerator.

Prepare the chocolate *crémeux*.
Heat another 1 lb. (500 g) of the pouring custard to 183°F (84°C). Chop the chocolate and melt it slowly in a bain-marie or in the microwave oven (on "defrost" or at 500 W maximum, stirring from time to time). Gradually pour one third of the hot custard over the melted chocolate. Using a flexible spatula, mix it in energetically, drawing small circles to create an elastic, shiny "kernel." Incorporate the second third of the custard, using the same procedure. Repeat with the last third and process briefly with an immersion blender. Pour the *crémeux* into the glasses or bowls, over the shortbread, and chill for 2 to 3 hours. When the *crémeux* has set, pour the coffee cream over it and chill again.

Just before serving, prepare the vanilla-scented Chantilly cream.
Pour the well-chilled cream into a mixing bowl. Slit the half vanilla bean lengthwise and scrape the seeds out into the cream. Add the sugar. Whip until the texture reaches that of a light Chantilly cream. Carefully place a dollop of vanilla-scented cream on top of the coffee cream and serve immediately.

Fresh Fruit Chocolate Bars

MAKES 2–3 BARS · PREPARATION TIME: 30 MINUTES · CHILLING TIME: 1 HOUR

INGREDIENTS

Bittersweet chocolate bars

7 oz. (200 g) bittersweet chocolate, 60 or 70 percent cocoa

2 ½ oz. (70 g) fresh raspberries or 2 ¼ oz. (60 g) fresh blueberries at room temperature

Milk chocolate bars

7 oz. (200 g) milk chocolate, 40 percent cocoa

2 ¼ oz. (60 g) fresh apricots, each cut into 6 pieces, at room temperature

EQUIPMENT

1 serrated knife

1 food processor fitted with a blade attachment (optional)

1 flexible spatula

1 kitchen thermometer

Chocolate bar molds

Temper the milk and bittersweet chocolates separately.

Using a chopping board, chop half the chocolate with a serrated knife. You may also use couverture chocolate in other forms, such as buttons, fèves, or pistoles. Finely chop the other half, or process it with the blade attachment of your food processor, and set it aside. Place the more coarsely chopped chocolate in a heatproof bowl.

If you have a double boiler, half-fill the bottom part with hot water. Otherwise, half-fill a pot or saucepan with hot water. Place the bowl in this, ensuring that it does not touch the bottom of the saucepan. Place the saucepan (or double boiler) over low heat and check that the water does not boil. Stir constantly. (You may also use the microwave oven, but only set at "defrost" or at 500 W maximum.) As soon as the chocolate begins to melt, stir it regularly using a flexible spatula so that it melts evenly.

Check the temperature with your thermometer. When it reaches 131°F–136°F (55°C–58°C) for the bittersweet chocolate and 113°F–122°F (45°C–50°C) for the milk chocolate, remove the chocolate from the double boiler and add the 3 ½ oz. (100 g) finely chopped chocolate, stirring until the bittersweet chocolate cools to 82°F–84°F (28°C–29°C) and the milk chocolate, to 81°F–82°F (27°C–28°C).

Briefly return the bowl to the double boiler to raise the temperature again. Remove after a few moments, and continue to stir until bittersweet chocolate reaches 88°F–90°F (31°C–32°C) and milk chocolate 84°F–86°F (29°C–30°C).

In a mixing bowl, quickly combine the fruit (at room temperature) with the tempered chocolate. Immediately spoon into the molds and give them a little shake to ensure that the surface is flat. Leave to rest for 1 hour in the refrigerator, turn out of the molds, and enjoy!

Coconut Bars

MAKES 4 BARS · PREPARATION TIME: 30 MINUTES · SETTING TIME: 48 HOURS

INGREDIENTS

14 oz. (400 g) white chocolate, 35 percent cocoa

White chocolate and coconut ganache

1 teaspoon plus heaped ½ teaspoon (¼ oz./8 g) grated
  unsweetened coconut
Scant ⅓ cup (70 ml) coconut milk
1 cup minus 2 tablespoons (220 ml) coconut liqueur,
  e.g. Malibu
1 heaped tablespoon (16 g) granulated sugar
5 ¼ oz. (145 g) white chocolate, 35 percent cocoa

EQUIPMENT

4 chocolate bar molds
1 flexible spatula
1 kitchen thermometer
1 piping bag

Two days ahead, temper the chocolate.

Temper 7 oz. (200 g) white chocolate using the method of your choice (see pp. 13–15).

Pour a thin layer of chocolate into the bar molds. Leave to set at room temperature.

Prepare the white chocolate and coconut ganache.

Lightly toast the grated coconut. Gently heat the coconut milk and liqueur. In a heavy-bottomed saucepan, cook the sugar until it forms a light caramel. When the caramel is ready, carefully pour in the heated coconut milk and liqueur, making sure it doesn't splash you.

Chop the white chocolate and melt it slowly in a bain-marie or in the microwave oven (on "defrost" or at 500 W maximum, stirring from time to time). Gradually pour one third of the coconut caramel over the melted chocolate. Using a flexible spatula, mix it in energetically, drawing small circles to create an elastic, shiny "kernel." Incorporate the second third of the liquid, using the same procedure. Repeat with the last third. Stir in the lightly toasted grated coconut.

When the ganache has cooled to 82°F (28°C), spoon it into a piping bag and partially fill the chocolate-lined molds; make sure that the ganache is no hotter than this when you fill the bars, otherwise the white chocolate will become "detempered." Ensure you leave a space of just under 1/16 in. (2 mm) below the rim so that you will be able to fit in the closing layer of the bar. Leave to set for 24 hours in a cool room.

The next day, finish the bars.

Temper the remaining 7 oz. (200 g) white chocolate and pour into the molds to enclose the filling. Leave to set for 24 hours in a cool room.

Golden *Palets*

MAKES ABOUT 50 *PALETS* · PREPARATION TIME: 40 MINUTES · SETTING TIME: 3 HOURS PLUS OVERNIGHT

INGREDIENTS
Bittersweet chocolate ganache
8 oz. (225 g) bittersweet chocolate, 70 percent cocoa
½ vanilla bean
¾ cup (200 ml) whipping cream
2 tablespoons (1 ½ oz./40 g) honey
3 tablespoons plus 1 teaspoon (1 ¾ oz./50 g) butter, diced

Coating and decoration
1 lb. (500 g) bittersweet chocolate, 70 percent cocoa
Edible gold leaf

EQUIPMENT
1 flexible spatula
1 kitchen thermometer
1 immersion blender
1 piping bag
1 silicone baking mat or 1 baking sheet
Parchment paper
An additional baking sheet
1 dipping fork
Sheets of food-safe acetate (optional)

A day ahead, prepare the bittersweet chocolate ganache.

Chop the chocolate and melt it slowly in a bain-marie or in the microwave oven (on "defrost" or at 500 W maximum, stirring from time to time).

Slit the half vanilla bean and scrape out the seeds. Place the whipping cream, honey, and vanilla seeds and bean in a saucepan and bring to a boil. Leave to infuse for a few minutes and strain.

Gradually pour a third of the boiling liquid over the melted chocolate. Using a flexible spatula, mix in energetically, drawing small circles to create an elastic, shiny "kernel." Incorporate the second third of the liquid, using the same procedure. Repeat with the last third. As soon as the ganache reaches a temperature of 95°F–104°F (35°C–40°C), incorporate the diced butter. Process briefly with an immersion blender until the mixture is completely emulsified. Leave to set for at least 3 hours.

Pipe out the ganache *palets*.

As soon as the ganache is thick enough to be piped out, fill a piping bag and pipe out small, truffle-sized balls onto a silicone mat or a baking sheet lined with parchment paper.

Place a sheet of parchment paper over the baking sheet of truffle balls and then place a baking sheet on top of this, pressing lightly to flatten the balls of ganache. This will create the *palet* shape. Remove the baking sheet and leave to set overnight.

Coat the ganache.

Line a baking sheet with a sheet of acetate if you have some, otherwise use parchment paper. Temper the chocolate using the method of your choice (see pp. 13–15).

Pour the tempered chocolate into a large mixing bowl. Very carefully peel off the sheet of paper protecting the ganache *palets*.

Place a *palet* on a dipping fork and dip into the tempered chocolate. Press the ganache down with the tines of the fork. Retrieve the *palet* with the fork and dip it three or four times to create the suction that will prevent the chocolate from forming a coating that is too thick. Then scrape on the edge of the mixing bowl so that the layer of chocolate left on the *palet* is thin. Carefully place the coated *palet* on the prepared baking sheet.

Place a small amount of gold leaf on each *palet* and leave to set. Cover each one, if possible, with a strip of food-safe acetate.

Exotic Fruit with Lime-Scented White Chocolate *Crémeux*

SERVES 6–8 · PREPARATION TIME: 1 HOUR 30 MINUTES
CHILLING TIME: OVERNIGHT · COOKING TIME: 10 MINUTES · RESTING TIME: 15 MINUTES

INGREDIENTS

Lime-scented white chocolate *crémeux*
Zest of 2 unwaxed limes
1 ½ sheets (3 g) gelatin
5 egg yolks
¼ cup (1 ¾ oz./50 g) granulated sugar
1 cup (250 ml) whole milk
1 cup (250 ml) whipping cream
8 oz. (225 g) white chocolate, 35 percent cocoa

Phyllo roses
5–6 sheets phyllo pastry
3 tablespoons plus 1 teaspoon (1 ¾ oz./50 g) butter
Confectioners' sugar for dusting

Exotic fruit salad
1 banana
½ grapefruit
½ pineapple
1 orange
1 mango

EQUIPMENT
1 whisk
1 kitchen thermometer
1 immersion blender
1 baking sheet
1 chinois (fine sieve)
1 flexible spatula
1 pastry brush

A day ahead, prepare the lime-scented white chocolate *crémeux*.

Finely chop the zest of the limes. Soften the gelatin in a bowl of cold water. While it is softening, whisk the egg yolks, sugar, and zest in a mixing bowl. Pour the mixture into a saucepan and add the milk and cream. Simmer gently, stirring constantly, until the mixture coats the back of a spoon. It should reach a temperature of 180°F–183°F (82°C–84°C). Remove from the heat and pour the custard into a deep mixing bowl. Process for a few seconds with an immersion blender for a smooth, creamy texture. Wring the water out of the gelatin and incorporate into the mixture, stirring until completely dissolved. Strain the custard through a chinois (fine sieve).

Chop the chocolate and melt it slowly in a bain-marie or in the microwave oven (on "defrost" or at 500 W maximum, stirring from time to time).

Gradually pour one third of the hot custard over the melted chocolate. Using a flexible spatula, mix in energetically, drawing small circles to create an elastic, shiny "kernel." Incorporate the second third of the liquid, using the same procedure. Repeat with the last third. Process with an immersion blender for a smooth, creamy texture. Chill overnight.

Prepare the phyllo pastry roses.
Preheat the oven to 350°F (180°C).

Unroll the sheets of phyllo pastry and cut each one in half. Crumple them up to give them some volume—they should look like a rose. Place them on a baking sheet and leave to dry out for about 15 minutes.

While they are drying out, melt the butter and then lightly brush the crumpled sheets of phyllo. Dust them generously with confectioners' sugar

and bake for a few minutes, until golden and lightly caramelized.

Peel the fruit and cut into fine dice. Arrange the diced fruit in soup plates, or other deep plates.

To serve, arrange a scoop of lime-scented white chocolate *crémeux* on each plate and garnish with a crisp phyllo rose at the last moment (so they don't go soggy in the syrup).

Cookies

MAKES ABOUT 30 COOKIES · PREPARATION TIME: 15 MINUTES
COOKING TIME: 12 MINUTES PER BAKING SHEET

INGREDIENTS

1 ½ sticks (6 ⅓ oz./180 g) unsalted butter
Scant ⅔ cup (4 ¼ oz./120 g) light brown sugar (*cassonade*)
1 egg
2 cups (6 ⅓ oz./180 g) cake flour
1 teaspoon plus 1 heaped ¼ teaspoon (5 g) baking powder
5 ½ oz. (150 g) chopped chocolate
5 ½ oz. (150 g) mixed nuts (pecans, macadamia, cashew, walnuts, etc.), roughly chopped
3 Carambar candies (a French caramel and cocoa toffee) or other similar long toffees, cut into pieces

EQUIPMENT

1 handheld electric beater
1 sieve
1 baking sheet lined with parchment paper.

Preheat the oven to 350°F (170°C). In a mixing bowl, soften the butter. Then, using an electric beater, cream it with the light brown sugar. Add the egg. Sift the flour and baking powder together into the mixture and incorporate. Stir in the chopped chocolate, nuts, and pieces of caramel and mix until thoroughly combined.

Shape small balls of dough, about 1 ½ in. (4 cm) in diameter. Place them on a lined baking sheet about 3 in. (8 cm) apart, and flatten them very gently; don't flatten them too much, so they will remain soft inside and crisp outside. Bake for about 12 minutes.

Dulcey Panna Cotta

MAKES 10 *VERRINES* · PREPARATION TIME: 40 MINUTES
CHILLING TIME: 45 MINUTES · COOKING TIME: 20 MINUTES

INGREDIENTS

Panna cotta
7 ½ oz. (210 g) Valrhona Dulcey chocolate, 32 percent cocoa
1 ½ teaspoons (10 g) glucose syrup
1 ¼ sheets (2.5 g) gelatin
½ cup (125 ml) milk
1 cup (250 ml) heavy cream

½ quantity almond streusel (see p. 187)

Mango–banana marmalade
6 ¾ oz. (190 g) mango
3 tablespoons (70 g) mango pulp
2 tablespoons (25 g) banana pulp
1 ½ tablespoons (20 g) brown sugar

Chocolate decorations
Valrhona Dulcey chocolate, 32 percent cocoa

EQUIPMENT
1 kitchen thermometer
1 chinois (fine sieve)
1 flexible spatula
1 immersion blender
1 baking sheet
1 rolling pin
2 sheets food-safe acetate
1 piping bag
10 shot glasses (*verrines*)

Prepare the panna cotta.

Melt the chocolate (see p. 10) to 104°F (40°C) and add the glucose.

Soften the gelatin in cold water. Bring the milk to a boil. Wring the water out of the gelatin and dissolve it into the milk. Strain through a chinois (fine sieve). Gradually pour it over the melted chocolate, briskly mixing it in, using a flexible spatula, with a small circular movement to create an elastic, shiny "kernel." Add the cold heavy cream to this mixture. Process with an immersion blender for a few seconds. Leave to set in the refrigerator.

Make the almond streusel.

Follow the recipe on p. 187, remembering to halve the quantities.

Prepare the mango–banana marmalade.

Peel and pit the mango and dice the flesh into pieces measuring ½ in. (1.5 cm). Put the mango pulp, banana pulp, and sugar into a pan and bring to a boil. Let cool, then add the diced mango and set aside in the refrigerator.

Make the Dulcey chocolate decorations.

Temper the Dulcey chocolate using the method of your choice (see pp. 13–15). Using a rolling pin, spread the tempered chocolate between two sheets of food-safe acetate to form two rectangles measuring ½ × 4 in. (1.5 × 10 cm).

To assemble, use a piping bag to pipe 1 oz. (30 g) of mango–banana marmalade into each glass, then put the glasses into the freezer for 5 minutes to freeze the surface of the marmalade. Spoon the panna cotta into each glass and refrigerate. When ready to serve, sprinkle some almond streusel into each glass and add the Dulcey chocolate decorations.

Creamy

Chocolate, Clementine, and Orange Blossom Water Tartlets

SERVES 6–8 · PREPARATION TIME: 1 HOUR · COOKING TIME: 20 MINUTES · CHILLING TIME: 3 HOURS

INGREDIENTS
Small quantity almond shortcrust
   pastry (see p. 186) or 1 package
   sweet pie crust

Milk chocolate–clementine *crémeux*
5 oz. (140 g) milk chocolate,
   40 percent cocoa
2 egg yolks
2 tablespoons (1 oz./25 g) granulated
   sugar
½ cup (125 ml) milk
½ cup (125 ml) whipping cream
Zest of 1 unwaxed or organic
   clementine

**Orange blossom–scented Chantilly
cream**
1 cup (250 ml) whipping cream, well
   chilled
¼ vanilla bean
2 tablespoons (1 oz./25 g) granulated
   sugar
A few drops of orange blossom water

EQUIPMENT
8 tartlet molds
1 rolling pin
2 sheets food-safe acetate or
   parchment paper
1 whisk or handheld electric beater
1 kitchen thermometer
1 sieve
1 immersion blender
1 flexible spatula
Plastic wrap
1 piping bag fitted with a plain tip

Prepare the almond shortcrust pastry (see p. 186), if using.

Alternatively, use store-bought sweet pie crust. Butter the tartlet molds. Roll the dough out to a thickness of ⅛ in. (3 mm) and line the tartlet molds. Chill for 30 minutes. Preheat the oven to 300°F–325°F (150°C–160°C) and bake for about 15 to 20 minutes, until the pastry is a nice golden color.

Prepare the chocolate–clementine *crémeux.*

Chop the chocolate and melt it slowly in a bain-marie or in the microwave oven (on "defrost" or at 500 W maximum, stirring from time to time). Whip the egg yolks and sugar together. Add the milk, cream, and grated clementine zest. Pour the mixture into a saucepan and cook over low heat, stirring constantly, until the mixture thickens slightly and coats the back of a spoon. The temperature should be 180°F–183°F (82°C–84°C). Remove from the heat and strain into a mixing bowl. Process for a few seconds with an immersion blender,

until the texture is smooth and creamy. Gradually pour one third of the hot custard over the melted chocolate. Using a flexible spatula, mix it in energetically, drawing small circles to create an elastic, shiny "kernel." Incorporate the second third of the custard, using the same procedure. Repeat with the last third. Pour it into a bowl, cover with plastic wrap flush with the surface, and chill.

When the tartlet shells are ready, pour in the chocolate–clementine *crémeux* and leave to set in the refrigerator for at least 2 hours.

Prepare the scented Chantilly cream.

Pour the well-chilled cream into a mixing bowl. Slit the quarter vanilla bean lengthwise and scrape the seeds out into the cream. Add the sugar and orange blossom water. Whip until the texture reaches that of a light Chantilly cream. Spoon the cream into a piping bag fitted with a plain tip and pipe out rounds of scented Chantilly cream on top of the tartlets.

Cilantro-Scented Pineapple and Mango Tart

SERVES 6–8 · PREPARATION TIME: 2 HOURS · FREEZING TIME: 30 MINUTES
COOKING TIME: 10–15 MINUTES · CHILLING TIME: 2 HOURS 30 MINUTES

INGREDIENTS
Chocolate–almond streusel
Scant cup (2 ⅔ oz./75 g) cake flour
1 ½ tablespoons (10 g) unsweetened
  cocoa powder
1 cup minus 1 tablespoon (2 ⅔ oz./75 g)
  ground blanched almonds
Generous ⅓ cup (2 ⅔ oz./75 g) light
  brown sugar (cassonade)
Generous pinch (3 g) fleur de sel
5 tablespoons plus 1 teaspoon
  (2 ⅔ oz./75 g) butter, chilled

Light ivory and passion fruit mousse
1 ½ sheets (3 g) gelatin
5 ½ oz. (150 g) white chocolate,
  35 percent cocoa
Scant ½ cup (90 ml) milk
Generous ½ cup (160 ml) whipping
  cream, well chilled
½ passion fruit

Garnish
½ pineapple
1 mango
A few sprigs of fresh cilantro
  (coriander)

EQUIPMENT
1 sieve
Cookie cutters, square or any other
  shape of your choice
1 baking sheet lined with parchment
  paper
1 flexible spatula
1 whisk or handheld electric beater
1 kitchen thermometer

Prepare the chocolate–almond streusel.
Sift the flour and cocoa powder together. Combine them with the ground almonds, brown sugar, and fleur de sel. Cut the chilled butter into small cubes and using your fingers mix it into the preparation until it forms a crumbly texture. Place in the freezer for at least 30 minutes.

Preheat the oven to 300°F–325°F (150°C–160°C). Place the cookie cutters on a lined baking sheet and spread the streusel mixture at the bases. If you wish to consolidate the crumbly mixture, lightly spray it with water before baking. Bake for about 10 to 15 minutes, until nicely browned. Leave to cool at room temperature.

Prepare the ivory and passion fruit mousse.
Soften the gelatin in a bowl of cold water.

Chop the chocolate and melt it slowly in a bain-marie or in the microwave oven (on "defrost" or at 500 W maximum, stirring from time to time).

Bring the milk to a boil in a saucepan. Wring the water out of the gelatin and incorporate it into the hot milk. Immediately remove from the heat.

Slowly pour one third of the hot milk over the melted chocolate. Using a flexible spatula, briskly mix it in with a small circular movement to create an elastic, shiny "kernel." Incorporate the second third of the hot milk, using the same procedure. Repeat with the last third.

Using either a whisk or an electric beater, lightly whip the well-chilled cream. When the milk, gelatin, and chocolate mixture has cooled to 86°F (30°C), carefully fold in the lightly whipped cream, incorporating the passion fruit seeds as well. As soon as the mixture is thoroughly combined, pour it into the cookie cutters over the cooled chocolate streusel. Chill for 1 to 2 hours.

Peel the pineapple and mango and cut them into differently sized cubes. Pick the leaves from the cilantro stalks and chop them finely. Combine the differently sized cubes of fruit in a mixing bowl and toss them with the chopped cilantro leaves.

Remove the cookie cutters from the layered desserts and garnish with the cilantro-flavored fruit cubes. Keep in the refrigerator until ready to serve.

Bittersweet Chocolate Mousse

SERVES 6–8 · PREPARATION TIME: 15 MINUTES · CHILLING TIME: 12 HOURS

INGREDIENTS
Chocolate mousse
10 ½ oz. (300 g) bittersweet chocolate, 70 percent cocoa
Scant ⅔ cup (150 ml) whipping cream
3 (2 ¼ oz./60 g) egg yolks
6–7 (7 oz./200 g) egg whites
¼ cup (1 ¾ oz./50 g) granulated sugar

Chocolate sauce
3 oz. (85 g) bittersweet chocolate, 70 percent cocoa
½ cup minus 2 tablespoons (100 ml) whole milk

EQUIPMENT
1 flexible spatula
1 whisk or handheld electric beater and, if possible,
   1 stand-alone mixer
1 kitchen thermometer
1 immersion blender

Prepare the chocolate mousse.
Chop the chocolate and melt it slowly in a bain-marie or in the microwave oven (on "defrost" or at 500 W maximum, stirring from time to time).

Bring the cream to a boil in a saucepan. As soon as it reaches a boil, remove from the heat. Slowly pour one third of the hot cream over the melted chocolate. Using a flexible spatula, briskly mix it in with a small circular movement to create an elastic, shiny "kernel." Incorporate the second third of the hot cream, using the same procedure. Repeat with the last third. Stir in the egg yolks until the mixture is perfectly smooth.

Whisk the egg whites, together with a little of the sugar, until they form soft peaks. When they reach this stage, mix in the remaining sugar and whisk until they are shiny. When the chocolate mixture has cooled to 113°F–122°F (45°C–50°C), fold in one quarter of the whisked egg whites to lighten the mixture, then carefully incorporate the remaining egg whites. Chill for 12 hours.

Prepare the chocolate sauce (see p. 33).

Thirty minutes before serving, remove the mousse from the refrigerator to bring it to room temperature. Serve with warm or chilled sauce.

Orange Blossom Ivory Mousse with a Praline Heart

SERVES 12 · PREPARATION TIME: 40 MINUTES · CHILLING TIME: 2 HOURS
COOKING TIME: 12 MINUTES · FREEZING TIME: 6 HOURS

INGREDIENTS

Almond–praline sponge
Generous ¼ cup (1 oz./25 g) cake flour
¾ teaspoon (3 g) baking powder
2 eggs
1 heaped tablespoon (1 oz./25 g) multi-floral honey
2 ½ tablespoons (1 oz./30 g) granulated sugar
1 ⅔ oz. (45 g) praline
Generous ⅓ cup (1 oz./30 g) ground blanched almonds
Scant ¼ cup (50 ml) whipping cream
2 tablespoons (1 oz./30 g) butter

Praline heart
½ sheet (1 g) gelatin
½ cup minus 1 ½ tablespoons (100 ml) whipping cream
4 ¼ oz. (150 g) praline

Orange blossom ivory mousse
4 ⅔ oz. (130 g) white chocolate, 35 percent cocoa
2 sheets (4 g) gelatin
Scant ⅓ cup (70 ml) whole milk
Scant ⅔ cup (150 ml) whipping cream, well chilled
1 teaspoon (5 ml) orange blossom water

Caramelized hazelnuts
Chocolate pearls

EQUIPMENT
1 sieve
1 whisk or handheld electric beater
1 kitchen thermometer
1 baking sheet lined with parchment paper or 1 silicone baking mat
1 ¼ in. (3 cm) diameter cookie cutter
1 piping bag
Silicone ice-cube tray (tray of 12)
1 flexible spatula
12 individual 1 ¼ in. (3 cm) diameter pastry rings

Prepare the almond–praline sponge.
Sift the flour and baking powder together. Combine the eggs, honey, and sugar. Mix in the praline, and then the ground almonds. Stir in the sifted dry ingredients. Heat the cream to 113°F–122°F (45°C–50°C) and incorporate the butter. Pour this cream–butter mixture into the batter. Chill for 2 hours.

Preheat the oven to 350°F (180°C). Pour the batter over a lined baking sheet or silicone baking mat and bake for about 12 minutes, until a cake tester or knife tip comes out dry. Leave to cool, then cut out disks using the cookie cutter.

Prepare the praline heart.
Soften the gelatin in a bowl of cold water. Bring the whipping cream to a boil in a saucepan, remove from the heat, wring the water from the gelatin, and incorporate it into the hot cream. Pour the cream over the praline by thirds, using the procedure outlined on p. 162. Spoon the praline mixture into a piping bag and pipe it out into 12 silicone ice-cube cavities. Freeze for a minimum of 3 hours.

Prepare the orange blossom ivory mousse.
Chop the chocolate and melt it slowly in a bain-marie or in the microwave oven (on "defrost" or at 500 W maximum, stirring from time to time). Soften the gelatin in a bowl of cold water. Bring the milk to a boil, remove from the heat, wring the water out of the gelatin, and incorporate it into the milk. Gradually pour the boiling milk over the melted chocolate, one third at a time, as on p. 162.

In a mixing bowl, whisk the cold cream until it is lightly whipped. When the chocolate mixture has cooled to 95°F–104°F (35°C–40°C), fold in the lightly whipped cream using a flexible spatula. Stir in the orange blossom water.

Assemble the desserts.
Place the individual pastry rings on a baking sheet lined with parchment paper. Place the sponge bases at the bottom of the rings. Turn the iced praline hearts out of the ice tray onto the sponge bases.

Then pour the orange blossom ivory mousse over the iced praline hearts and freeze for 3 hours.

Remove the rings and decorate with a few caramelized hazelnuts and some chocolate pearls.

Chocolate Mousse and Creamy Caramel in a Spoon

SERVES 6–8 · PREPARATION TIME: 1 HOUR 30 MINUTES · CHILLING TIME: OVERNIGHT

INGREDIENTS

Chocolate mousse

6 ⅓ oz. (180 g) bittersweet chocolate, 60 percent cocoa
1 ½ sheets (3 g) gelatin
⅔ cup (170 ml) whole milk
1 ½ cups (350 ml) whipping cream, well chilled

Creamy caramel sauce

¾ cup (200 ml) whipping cream
1 tablespoon (20 g) honey
Scant ½ cup (3 ¼ oz./90 g) granulated sugar

(Alternatively, use 1 jar caramel spread, preferably
  salted caramel)

Nuts or dried fruit of your choice

EQUIPMENT

1 flexible spatula
1 whisk or handheld electric beater
1 kitchen thermometer
8 Chinese-style soup spoons for serving

A day ahead, prepare the chocolate mousse.

Chop the chocolate and melt it slowly in a bain-marie or in the microwave oven (on "defrost" or at 500 W maximum, stirring from time to time).

Soften the gelatin in a bowl of very cold water. Bring the milk to a boil in a saucepan. Immediately remove from the heat. Wring the water out of the gelatin and incorporate it into the hot milk.

Slowly pour one third of the hot milk over the melted chocolate. Using a flexible spatula, briskly mix it in with a small circular movement to create an elastic, shiny "kernel." Incorporate the second third of the hot milk, using the same procedure. Repeat with the last third.

Using a whisk or an electric beater, whisk the well-chilled cream until it forms soft peaks—it should be softly whipped. When the chocolate mixture has cooled to 95°F–113°F (35°C–45°C)—the cream will melt otherwise—carefully fold in the softly whipped cream with a flexible spatula. Chill overnight.

The next day, prepare the creamy caramel sauce, if making.

Bring the cream to a boil in a small saucepan. In a large saucepan, melt the honey, then gradually pour in the sugar, stirring constantly until you obtain a light caramel. Slowly pour in the hot cream, taking care that the caramel does not sputter, and bring the mixture to 217°F (103°C). Leave to cool to room temperature.

Place small scoops of the mousse in Chinese-style soup spoons and drizzle with creamy caramel sauce or caramel spread. Sprinkle with nuts or dried fruit.

Pear and Milk Chocolate Petits Fours

SERVES 6–8 · PREPARATION TIME: 1 HOUR 30 MINUTES
COOKING TIME: 10 MINUTES · FREEZING TIME: 3 HOURS 30 MINUTES

INGREDIENTS

Small quantity almond shortcrust
 pastry (see p. 186) or 1 package
 sweet pie crust

Chocolate–caramel–vanilla mousse

3 ½ oz. (100 g) milk chocolate,
 40 percent cocoa
½ vanilla bean
1 sheet (2 g) gelatin
2 ½ tablespoons (1 oz./30 g)
 granulated sugar
2 egg yolks
1 cup (250 ml) whipping cream, divided
 as follows: 4 tablespoons (50 ml)
 plus ¾ cup (200 ml)

Lemon-scented crushed pear

1 pear
Juice of ½ lemon
A little granulated sugar

Caramel and white chocolate glaze

9 ⅓ oz. (265 g) white chocolate,
 35 percent cocoa
2 sheets (4 g) gelatin
¾ cup (175 ml) whipping cream
3 tablespoons (40 ml) water
1 ½ tablespoons (1 oz./30 g) glucose
 syrup
¼ cup (1 ¾ oz./50 g) granulated sugar
1 tablespoon plus 2 teaspoons (25 ml)
 grape-seed oil

EQUIPMENT

1 rolling pin
2 sheets food-safe acetate
1 baking sheet lined with parchment
 paper
1 kitchen thermometer
1 flexible spatula
1 immersion blender
1 whisk
Small square silicone molds
1 food processor

**Prepare the almond shortcrust pastry
(see p. 186), if using.**

Alternatively, use store-bought sweet pie crust. Preheat the oven to 300°F–325°F (150°C–160°C). Cut squares of pastry slightly smaller than your molds. Place them on a baking sheet lined with parchment paper and bake for about 10 minutes.

Prepare the chocolate–caramel–vanilla mousse.

Chop the chocolate and melt it (see p. 10). Slit the half vanilla bean and scrape out the seeds. Soften the gelatin in a bowl filled with cold water. Cook the sugar in a saucepan until it forms a light caramel (the temperature should be 343°F–347°F/173°C–175°C). While it is cooking, beat the egg yolks. Carefully stir 4 tablespoons (50 ml) whipping cream into the caramelized sugar. Pour the liquid over the beaten egg yolks, add the vanilla seeds, and return to the heat. Stir until it thickens and coats the back of a spoon. Wring the excess water from the gelatin and incorporate it into the custard. Process for a few seconds with an immersion blender until smooth and creamy. Incorporate the hot custard into the melted chocolate by thirds, following the procedure on p. 162. Process briefly again until completely emulsified. In a mixing bowl, lightly whip the remaining ¾ cup whipping cream. When the chocolate–custard mixture has cooled to 113°F–122°F (45°C–50°C), fold in one third of the lightly whipped cream. Then carefully fold in the remaining cream using a flexible spatula. Pour the mousse into the small molds and top with a small square of baked shortcrust pastry. Freeze for about 3 hours.

Prepare the lemon-scented crushed pear.

Peel and core the pear. Cut into pieces and place in a food processor. Pour in the lemon juice and process. Adjust the taste, adding a touch of sugar if necessary.

When the mousses are completely frozen, remove them from their molds and turn them upside down. Top them with a little crushed pear. Return to the freezer for 30 minutes.

Prepare the caramel and white chocolate glaze.
Chop the chocolate and melt it (see p. 10). Soften the gelatin in a bowl of cold water. In a saucepan, heat the whipping cream, water, and glucose syrup. Remove from the heat, wring the water from the gelatin, and incorporate it into the hot liquid. Place the sugar in a heavy-bottomed saucepan. Cook until it forms a light caramel, then pour it into the cream and glucose syrup mixture. Pour this hot cream gradually over the melted chocolate by thirds, according to the procedure on p. 162. Stir in the grape-seed oil. Process, ensuring you do not incorporate any air bubbles. Cover the petits fours with the glaze and chill until ready to serve.

Mister Clown

SERVES 8 · PREPARATION TIME: 1 HOUR 30 MINUTES
COOKING TIME: 10 MINUTES · FREEZING TIME: 4 HOURS

INGREDIENTS

Chocolate cake
1 ¼ oz. (35 g) bittersweet chocolate, 60 percent cocoa
4 tablespoons (2 ¼ oz./60 g) butter
Scant cup (2 ¾ oz./80 g) cake flour
1 ¼ teaspoons (5 g) baking powder
2 tablespoons (½ oz./15 g) unsweetened cocoa powder
3 eggs
2 ½ tablespoons (1 ¾ oz./50 g) honey
Scant ½ cup (2 ¾ oz./80 g) granulated sugar
Generous ½ cup (1 ¾ oz./50 g) ground blanched almonds
⅓ cup (80 ml) whipping cream

Bittersweet chocolate Chantilly mousse (see p. 189)
6 ⅓ oz. (180 g) bittersweet chocolate, 60 percent cocoa
1 ¼ cups (300 ml) whipping cream, divided as follows:
  ¾ cup (200 ml) plus ½ cup (100 ml)

Crunchy almond coating
2 ½ oz. (70 g) chopped almonds
10 ½ oz. (300 g) bittersweet chocolate, 60 percent cocoa
2 tablespoons (30 ml) grape-seed oil

Decoration
White and bittersweet chocolate, melted
Various fruit coulis, store-bought or homemade

EQUIPMENT
1 sieve
1 whisk or handheld electric beater
1 confectionery frame or rectangular cake mold,
  9 ½ × 13 ½ in. (24 × 34 cm)
1 baking sheet lined with parchment paper or 1 baking mat
8 pastry rings, 3 in. (7 ½ cm) diameter
1 flexible spatula
1 kitchen thermometer
2 paper decorating cones

Prepare the chocolate cake batter.
Using the ingredients and quantities given above, follow the method on p. 22. Place the rectangular frame on a lined baking sheet, or use a cake pan. Pour the batter into the pan or frame and bake at 350°F (180°C) for about 8 to 10 minutes, until a knife tip or cake tester comes out dry.

Leave to cool, then cut out eight disks the same size as the pastry rings.

Prepare the chocolate Chantilly mousse.
Using the quantities given above, follow the recipe on p. 189.

Assemble the cake.
Place the individual pastry rings on a baking sheet lined with parchment paper. In each one, place a disk of chocolate sponge and cover it with a layer of chocolate Chantilly mousse about 1 in. (2–3 cm) thick. Freeze for about 4 hours. Remove the rings from around these little *palets* and return them to the freezer.

Prepare the crunchy almond coating.
Heat the oven to 325°F (160°C) and roast the chopped almonds for a few minutes. Leave to cool. Melt the chocolate over a bain-marie or in the microwave oven (on "defrost" or at 500 W, stirring from time to time). Stir in the oil and then the roasted almonds.

Insert the tip of a kitchen knife into the chocolate sponge to lift it up and dip it, still frozen, into the crunchy coating. Remove immediately, allowing the excess coating to drip off, and then place each cake on a serving plate.

Prepare two paper decorating cones and fill one with melted bittersweet chocolate and the other with melted white chocolate. Draw the eyes and mouth on the top of the chocolate cake using the white chocolate, and with the bittersweet chocolate draw the bodies of the clowns on the plates. Place the fruit coulis in bowls, and using brushes or—even better—pipettes, the children can then decorate their clowns using the various fruit coulis.

Glasgow Cakes

MAKES 16 SMALL OVAL CAKES · PREPARATION TIME: 45 MINUTES
COOKING TIME: 45 MINUTES · SOAKING TIME: 1 HOUR 30 MINUTES · FREEZING TIME: OVERNIGHT

INGREDIENTS

Raisins soaked in whiskey
Scant ½ cup (100 ml) whiskey
4 ¼ oz. (120 g) golden raisins

Almond *dacquoise*
⅓ cup (1 oz./30 g) cake flour
1 cup (3 oz./85 g) blanched ground almonds
¾ cup (3 ½ oz./100 g) confectioners' sugar
3 egg whites
¼ cup (1 ¾ oz./50 g) granulated sugar

Custard-based bittersweet chocolate mousse
5 ¾ oz. (165 g) bittersweet chocolate, 70 percent cocoa
1 egg yolk
1 heaped tablespoon (15 g) sugar
⅓ cup minus 1 teaspoon (75 ml) whole milk
1 ¼ cups (300 ml) whipping cream, divided as follows:
  ⅓ cup minus 1 teaspoon (75 ml) and 1 cup minus
  1 ½ tablespoons (225 ml)

Whiskey whipped cream
Generous ¾ cup (200 ml) whipping cream
2 ½ tablespoons (⅔ oz./20 g) confectioners' sugar
1 tablespoon plus 2 teaspoons (25 ml) whiskey

EQUIPMENT
1 sieve
1 whisk or handheld electric beater
1 flexible spatula
1 jelly (Swiss) roll pan lined with parchment paper or
  1 silicone baking mat
1 baking sheet lined with parchment paper
1 kitchen thermometer
1 immersion blender
16 small oval silicone molds, length approx. 3 in. (7 cm)

A day ahead, prepare the whiskey-soaked raisins.

Bring the whiskey to a boil and pour it immediately over the golden raisins. Cover and leave them to plump for about 1 hour 30 minutes.

Prepare the almond *dacquoise*.

Preheat the oven to 350°F–375°F (180°C–190°C). Sift the flour with the ground almonds and the confectioners' sugar into a mixing bowl. Begin whisking the egg whites with the granulated sugar, until soft peaks form. Carefully fold in the sifted dry ingredients with a flexible spatula. Spread it out evenly over the lined jelly (Swiss) roll pan or silicone mat, setting aside 2 tablespoons of batter for decoration. Bake for about 10 minutes, until it turns a nice golden color. When cool, cut out 16 *dacquoise* bases just slightly smaller than the size of the molds.

Lower the oven temperature to 250°F (120°C). Spread out 16 teardrop shapes of the remaining *dacquoise* batter on a lined baking sheet. Bake for

about 35 minutes. Leave to cool and store in an airtight container.

Prepare the custard-based chocolate mousse.

Chop the chocolate and melt it slowly in a bain-marie or in the microwave oven (on "defrost" or at 500 W maximum, stirring from time to time).

In a mixing bowl, beat the egg yolk with the sugar until thick and pale. Pour this mixture into a saucepan, add the milk and ⅓ cup minus 1 teaspoon (75 ml) whipping cream, and simmer over low heat. The liquid should thicken slightly and coat the back of a spoon. The temperature should be 180°F–183°F (82°C–84°C). Remove from the heat and pour the custard into a deep mixing bowl. Process for a few seconds with an immersion blender to obtain a smooth, creamy texture.

Gradually pour one third of the hot custard over the melted chocolate. Using a flexible spatula, mix it in energetically, drawing small circles to create an elastic, shiny "kernel." Incorporate the second

third of the custard, using the same procedure. Repeat with the last third. Process with an immersion blender for a smooth, creamy texture.

Using a whisk or an electric beater, whip 1 cup minus 1 ½ tablespoons (225 ml) well-chilled cream until it is just lightly whipped. When the chocolate custard reaches a temperature of 113°F–122°F (45°C–50°C), fold in one third of the softly whipped cream. Carefully fold in the remaining cream with a flexible spatula.

Pour the mousse into the molds and divide the whiskey-soaked raisins evenly over the mousse, keeping some for garnish. Place the *dacquoise* bases on top of the mousse. Freeze overnight.

The next day, prepare the whiskey whipped cream.
Whip the cream with the confectioners' sugar until it just forms a Chantilly consistency. Add the whiskey and whip further if the cream is too liquid.

Turn the cakes out of their molds and decorate with the whiskey Chantilly cream, the remaining raisins, and a teardrop of *dacquoise*.

Chocolate Crown with Winter Fruit and Nuts

SERVES 8 · PREPARATION TIME: 45 MINUTES · CHILLING TIME: 12 HOURS

INGREDIENTS

Bittersweet chocolate mousse
10 ½ oz. (300 g) bittersweet chocolate, 70 percent cocoa
⅔ cup (150 ml) whipping cream
3 (2 ¼ oz./60 g) egg yolks
6–7 (7 oz./200 g) egg whites
¼ cup (1 ¾ oz./50 g) granulated sugar

Garnish
1 oz. (25 g) walnuts
1 oz. (25 g) unpeeled whole almonds
1 oz. (25 g) peeled whole hazelnuts

½ oz. (15 g) pine nuts, preferably Mediterranean
1 Reinette apple or Cox's Orange Pippin
1 pear, not too ripe
1 cup (250 ml) whipping cream
Scant ½ cup (2 ¾ oz./80 g) sugar
2 tablespoons (30 ml) water

EQUIPMENT

1 flexible spatula
1 whisk or handheld electric beater
1 kitchen thermometer
1 piping bag

A day ahead, prepare the chocolate mousse.
Chop the chocolate and melt it slowly in a bain-marie or in the microwave oven (on "defrost" or at 500 W maximum, stirring from time to time).

Bring the cream to a boil in a saucepan. As soon as it reaches a boil, remove from the heat. Slowly pour one third of the hot cream over the melted chocolate. Using a flexible spatula, briskly mix it in with a small circular movement to create an elastic, shiny "kernel." Incorporate the second third of the hot cream, using the same procedure. Repeat with the last third. Stir in the egg yolks until the mixture is smooth.

In the meantime, start whisking the egg whites with a little of the sugar. When they form soft peaks, incorporate the remaining sugar. When the chocolate mixture reaches 113°F–122°F (45°C–50°C), fold in one quarter of the whisked egg whites, then carefully fold in the rest. Chill the mousse for 12 hours.

The next day, prepare the garnish.
Roughly chop the nuts. Peel, core, and finely dice the apple and the pear. Heat a scant ¼ cup (50 ml) cream in a saucepan. Place the sugar and water in a heavy-bottomed saucepan and cook until it forms a caramel (the temperature should be 343°F–347°F/173°C–175°C). Remove the saucepan from the heat, and being careful not to splash yourself, pour in the hot cream. Leave to simmer for a few moments. Add the diced apple and bring back to a gentle simmer, then add the diced pear and roughly chopped nuts. Leave to chill in the refrigerator so that the nuts can soften and absorb all the aromas of the caramel.

In a mixing bowl, lightly whip the remaining ¾ cup (200 ml) well-chilled cream.

Assemble the dessert.
Spoon the mousse into a piping bag and pipe out rounds onto the plates. Serve with the caramelized fruit and nuts and a dollop of whipped cream on top.

White Chocolate Mousse with Strawberry Cloud

SERVES 8 · PREPARATION TIME: 50 MINUTES · CHILLING TIME: 6 HOURS · FREEZING TIME: 1 HOUR

INGREDIENTS

Homemade strawberry coulis
1 lb. 5 oz. (600 g) strawberries
⅓ cup (2 ¼ oz./60 g) granulated sugar
Juice of ½ lemon

Strawberry cloud
1 ½ sheets (3 g) gelatin
10 ½ oz. (300 g) homemade strawberry coulis (see above)

Lemon and white chocolate mousse
1 sheet (2 g) gelatin
5 ¼ oz. (150 g) white chocolate, 35 percent cocoa
⅓ cup (80 ml) soy milk

Zest of 1 unwaxed lemon
⅔ cup (160 ml) soy cream

Strawberry brunoise
5 oz. (140 g) strawberries
A little granulated sugar

EQUIPMENT
1 blender
1 chinois (fine sieve)
1 flexible spatula
1 kitchen thermometer
1 whisk
8 shot glasses (*verrines*)
1 siphon

Prepare the homemade strawberry coulis.
Hull the strawberries, wash them, dry them carefully, and blend them with the sugar and lemon juice. Taste to see if extra sugar is required. Strain through a chinois (fine sieve) and weigh out 10 ½ oz. (300 g) for the strawberry cloud.

Prepare the strawberry cloud.
Soften the gelatin in a bowl of cold water. Heat the measured strawberry coulis. Wring the excess water out of the gelatin and add it to the hot coulis. Stir until dissolved and chill for 2 hours.

Prepare the lemon and white chocolate mousse.
Soften the gelatin in a bowl of cold water. Chop the chocolate and melt it slowly in a bain-marie or in the microwave oven (on "defrost" or at 500 W maximum, stirring from time to time). Bring the soy milk to a boil in a saucepan, add the lemon zest and leave to infuse for 5 minutes. Strain, wring the water from the gelatin and dissolve it in the hot soy milk. Gradually pour one third of the hot liquid over the melted chocolate. Using a flexible spatula, mix it in energetically, drawing small circles to create an elastic, shiny "kernel." Incorporate the second third of the liquid, using the same procedure. Repeat with the last third. Leave to cool.

In a mixing bowl, whisk the soy cream until it thickens and is lightly whipped. When the chocolate mixture has cooled to 95°F–104°F (35°C–40°C), carefully fold in the whipped soy cream.

Prepare the strawberry brunoise.
Hull the strawberries, setting aside a few for decoration, if you wish. Finely dice the strawberries to make a brunoise and add a little sugar if necessary.

Assemble the dessert.
Carefully pour the strawberry coulis into the glasses. Place in the freezer for 1 hour. Pour the lemon and white chocolate mousse over the set coulis. Chill for 4 hours. Spoon the strawberry cloud mixture into the siphon. Arrange the strawberry brunoise over the mousse in each glass. Just before serving, press out some strawberry foam from the siphon into each glass. Decorate, if you wish, with some remaining strawberry brunoise or a halved strawberry.

Conclusion

The Valrhona Cité du Chocolat: a tribute to the chocolate that makes us melt with pleasure.

The Valrhona Cité du Chocolat is a fun, multi-sensory visitor center that provides a true tasting experience.

Valrhona created the Cité du Chocolat at Tain l'Hermitage, in southeastern France, on the historic site of its chocolate factory, with the aim of sharing its wealth of expertise and knowledge relating to fine chocolate-making.

Here, in a unique setting designed around taste, touch, and materials, visitors can discover everything about the world of cocoa and chocolate through interactive experiences that appeal to all five senses—from listening to the delicate sound of a spoon sinking into a chocolate mousse, to feeling the ridged shell of the fruit of a cacao tree, or from smelling the aromatic scents of the various ingredients used in chocolate-making, to observing and reproducing the artisans' techniques, and, of course, tasting chocolates of every shape and color.

The Valrhona Cité du Chocolat allows visitors to explore all the sumptuousness of chocolate and its myriad uses, and to take away with them a few secrets gleaned from this great purveyor of fine chocolate.

Basic
Recipes

Almond Paste

INGREDIENTS
2 tablespoons (1 ½ oz./40 g) honey
⅔ oz. (20 g) glucose syrup
6 tablespoons (90 ml) water
Scant cup (6 ⅓ oz./180 g) sugar
13 oz. (375 g) whole blanched almonds

EQUIPMENT
1 food processor fitted with a blade attachment
1 kitchen thermometer
1 sheet food-safe acetate or parchment paper

In a saucepan, bring the honey, glucose syrup, water, and sugar to a boil.

Process the almonds in the bowl of a food processor and add the boiling syrup. Process until the mixture reaches the consistency of a paste. The temperature should be 175°F (80°C).

Place on a sheet of food-safe acetate or parchment paper and continue mixing for a few minutes using a spoon or spatula, until the mixture is completely smooth.

Store the paste in an airtight container in the refrigerator for up to 2 months.

Almond Shortcrust Pastry

INGREDIENTS
Small quantity
1 stick (4 oz./115 g) unsalted butter, at room temperature, plus a little extra for the mold or cake pan
1 pinch table salt
⅔ cup (3 ¼ oz./90 g) confectioners' sugar
3 tablespoons (½ oz./15 g) ground blanched almonds
1 egg
Cake flour, divided as follows: ⅔ cup (2 oz./60 g) plus 2 cups (6 ⅓ oz./180 g)

Large quantity
1 ½ sticks (6 ⅓ oz./180 g) unsalted butter, at room temperature, plus a little extra for the mold or cake pan
1 pinch table salt
1 cup (5 oz./140 g) confectioners' sugar
Generous ½ cup, (1 ¾ oz./50 g) ground blanched almonds
1 egg
Cake flour, divided as follows: 1 cup (3 ¼ oz./90 g) plus 3 cups (9 ½ oz./270 g)

EQUIPMENT
1 rolling pin
2 sheets food-safe acetate

In a mixing bowl, soften the butter and mix with the salt, confectioners' sugar, ground almonds, egg, and the first (smaller) quantity of cake flour.

As soon as the ingredients are mixed through, add the remaining flour and mix until just combined.

Roll the dough out to a thickness of ⅛ in. (3 mm) between two sheets of acetate and chill it for about 30 minutes, ensuring that it is completely flat.

When the dough has hardened, peel off the sheets of acetate. Cut the dough out to the desired shape. Line the tart molds or leave flat if your recipe calls for this.

Chill for 30 minutes.

Preheat the oven to 300°F–325°F (150°C–160°C). Bake according to recipe instructions.

Almond Streusel

INGREDIENTS
Generous ½ cup (1 ¾ oz./50 g) cake flour, sifted
Generous ½ cup, (1 ¾ oz./50 g) ground blanched almonds
2 ¼ tablespoons (1 ¾ oz./50 g) molasses sugar, soft dark brown sugar, or Demerara sugar
Generous pinch (3 g) fleur de sel or salt
3 ½ tablespoons (1 ¾ oz./50 g) butter, well chilled

EQUIPMENT
1 baking sheet
Frying basket (optional)

Combine the flour, ground almonds, sugar, and fleur de sel or salt in a mixing bowl. Cut the chilled butter into small cubes, and mix it into the preparation, using your fingers, until it forms a crumbly texture. Place in the freezer for at least 30 minutes.

Preheat the oven to 300°F–325°F (150°C–160°C).

Spread the crumbs out onto a baking sheet and bake for about 10 to 15 minutes, until nicely browned. Leave to cool.

Chef's notes
If you prefer more regularly shaped streusel crumbs, form the mixture into a ball before chilling, and then push it through a frying basket.

Streusel crumbs may be frozen raw or baked. If baked, heat them in the oven to restore their original crunch.

Spiced Dough

INGREDIENTS
1 stick (4 oz./115 g) butter
2 ¾ cups (9 oz./250 g) cake flour
½ teaspoon ground cinnamon
⅔ cup (4 ½ oz./125 g) light brown sugar
⅓ cup (2 ⅔ oz./75 g) granulated sugar
½ egg, beaten
4 teaspoons (20 ml) whole milk

EQUIPMENT
1 flexible spatula
1 whisk or handheld electric beater (optional)
Plastic wrap
Rolling pin
2 sheets food-safe acetate

Take the butter out of the refrigerator several hours before you begin baking and place it in a mixing bowl. Mix it energetically with a flexible spatula.

Soften it further with the spatula or a whisk (the final texture is known as *beurre pommade*).

Preheat the oven to 350°F (170°C).

Sift the flour with the cinnamon and set aside.

Add the brown sugar and white granulated sugar to the butter and mix in well. Incorporate the egg and sifted flour and cinnamon. Lastly, stir in the milk and mix until the dough is smooth.

Cover the dough in plastic wrap and chill for about 1 hour.

Roll the dough out, preferably between two sheets of acetate, to a thickness of just under 1/16 in. (2 mm) and cut it out to fit the molds.

Bake for about 15 minutes and leave to cool.

Breton Shortbread

INGREDIENTS
1 cup plus scant ¼ cup (4 ¼ oz./120 g) all-purpose flour
1 teaspoon (4 g) baking powder
1 pinch salt
2 egg yolks
Scant ½ cup (2 ¾ oz./80 g) sugar
5 ½ tablespoons (2 ¾ oz./80 g) butter, softened

EQUIPMENT
1 handheld electric beater
1 rolling pin
2 sheets food-safe acetate or parchment paper
1 baking sheet

Preheat the oven to 350°F (170°C).

Sift the flour with the baking powder and the salt. Beat the egg yolks with the sugar until the mixture is thick and pale. Soften the butter and incorporate it, then the sifted dry ingredients. Roll out the dough, between two sheets of acetate if possible, to a thickness of ¼ in. (5 mm). Chill for 30 minutes.

Remove the dough from the refrigerator and cut out small ½ in. (1 cm) cubes. Place them on a baking sheet and bake for about 15 minutes, until a nice gold color.

Leave to cool.

Pistachio or Hazelnut Paste

INGREDIENTS
7 oz. (200 g) green pistachios or peeled hazelnuts
2 tablespoons (30 ml) grape-seed oil

EQUIPMENT
1 food processor fitted with a blade attachment

Preheat the oven to 300°F–325°F (150°C–160°C). Roast the nuts for about 10 minutes. Remove from the oven and allow to cool.

Pour the cooled nuts into the bowl of a food processor with the grape-seed oil. Process until the paste reaches a smooth consistency.

Store in an airtight container in the refrigerator for up to 3 weeks, or freeze in small quantities.

Chocolate Chantilly Mousse

INGREDIENTS

Weigh the chocolate according to its cocoa content:
Either 11 ¼ oz. (320 g) bittersweet chocolate,
  70 percent cocoa
Or 12 ¾ oz. (360 g) bittersweet chocolate, 60 percent cocoa
Or 14 oz. (400 g) milk chocolate, 40 percent cocoa
Or 1 lb. (450 g) white chocolate, 35 percent cocoa, plus
  3 sheets (6 g) gelatin
Well-chilled whipping cream, divided as follows: 1 ¾ cups
  (400 ml) plus generous ¾ cup (200 ml)

EQUIPMENT

1 whisk or handheld electric beater
1 flexible spatula
1 kitchen thermometer

Chop the chocolate and melt slowly in a bain-marie or in the microwave oven (on "defrost" or at 500 W maximum, stirring from time to time).

For a white chocolate mousse, soften the gelatin in a bowl of very cold water.

Using a whisk or a handheld electric beater, whip the first (larger) quantity of chilled cream until it is lightly whipped. Set aside in the refrigerator.

Heat the second (smaller) quantity of whipping cream in a saucepan to a simmer. Remove from the heat, squeeze the water from the gelatin sheets, if using, and incorporate them until just dissolved. Slowly pour one third of the hot mixture over the melted chocolate. Using a flexible spatula, briskly mix it in with a small circular movement to create an elastic, shiny "kernel." Then incorporate another third of the hot liquid, using the same circular motion, and finally, the last third, still mixing with a circular movement. Check the temperature at this stage: it should be 113°F–122°F (45°C–50°C), whatever type of chocolate you use, so that the chocolate does not harden into little chips when you incorporate the cream.

Carefully fold in the lightly whipped cream with a flexible spatula.

Use according to recipe instructions.

Alternatively, if serving alone, chill for about 12 hours. Remove from the refrigerator 1 hour before serving to bring it to room temperature.

This mousse keeps for 2 days in the refrigerator, and freezes well.

Index